THE WALTER LYNWOOD FLEMING
LECTURES IN SOUTHERN HISTORY

LOUISIANA STATE UNIVERSITY

WILLIAM B. HESSELTINE

Confederate Leaders

in the

New South

GREENWOOD PRESS, PUBLISHERS
WESTPORT, CONNECTICUT

Preface

NORTHERN propaganda in the Civil War pictured the leaders of the Southern Confederacy as members of a planter class living on their remote plantations surrounded by their colored menials and engaged in a slaveholders' conspiracy with a "diabolic" unity of purpose. Actually, as the internal history of the Confederacy bore ample evidence, the South's leaders, both military and civil, came from varied backgrounds and were united neither on secession, the conduct of the war, nor the purposes of the Confederacy. Conflicting ideas and personal rivalries harassed the brief existence of the Confederate States of America.

Military defeat and the collapse of the Confederate government did not bring an end to the confusion of counsel. While the Northern victors experimented with various devices to "reconstruct" the South, the former leaders of the Confederacy, faced with the political, economic, and social collapse of their system, made varying adjustments to new conditions. Some fled in terror of a conqueror's vengeance; some, with eager subservience, welcomed the victor.

In time most of them tended to align themselves in the opposing camps of Robert E. Lee, who became a symbol of those who built a New South, and Jefferson Davis, who clung tenaciously to the values and practices of the Old South.

These lectures, based upon a study of the postwar careers of 585 "leaders" of the Confederacy, explore primarily the opinions and activities of three groups of high-placed Confederates: the ministers, who sought to maintain or adapt the South's religious heritage; the educators, who faced the problem of training new generations of Southern leaders; and the industrial "managers" of mines and mills and railroads, who built a New South. They give only a casual glance at other groups—the farmers, bankers, authors, insurance men, engineers, and politicians—among the former leaders of the Confederacy. But the ministers, educators, and industrialists illustrate the problems of adjustment which the South's leaders —and the Southern people—faced after Appomattox. They illustrate, too, how the contending programs of Davis and Lee eventually produced a working compromise but left lasting divisions in the land of Dixie.

Perhaps the story is, as well, a case study in a recurrent problem in history. At times leaders of a defeated people have been killed by the victors; at other times they have been enslaved. Perhaps the apostles of Jefferson Davis would have contended that the latter fate befell the Confederacy's leaders, while men of the Lee tradition might sometimes have argued that the conquered Confederacy, like Greece, led captive her captors. But certainly the South's leaders, whether submissive or stubborn, wove strong threads of Confederate tradition into the fabric of American life.

Materials for this study have been scattered and fragmentary. Not even an adequate roster of Confederate civil and military leaders exists. Only A. J. Hanna, who traced the Confederate cabinet members' *Flight into Oblivion,* has attempted a systematic study of any group of Confederate leaders after the war. The leaders themselves wrote hundreds of reminiscent memoirs, but seldom did they remember to mention their postwar careers. Hundreds of biographies, ranging from tomes of fatuous praise to studies of critical scholarship, have been written about the Confederacy's leading men; but, with few exceptions, they end substantially with Appomattox. Even obituary notices and funeral sermons of prominent Confederates who were important civic leaders dwelt at length upon the deceaseds' military records and slighted their years in the New South. Many an industrial leader whose significant contribution was made after the Stars and Bars were furled was laid to rest clad in his Confederate uniform and with his rank, "C.S.A.," carved upon his gravestone.

For aid in ferreting out the obscured details—

from county histories, biographical dictionaries, newspaper files, and manuscript collections—I am primarily indebted to Mrs. Elizabeth Twaddell Pope, sometime research assistant in the University of Wisconsin. Mrs. Pope also generously gave me access to the notes for her forthcoming study of the "rebel brigadiers" in Congress. My thanks are due, too, to the Research Committee of the Graduate School of the University of Wisconsin, who supported this study, in part, from special funds voted by the state legislature; to my wife, who took notes and transcribed an execrable handwriting beyond the call of uxorial duty; and to the officials of the University of Wisconsin Library, the Wisconsin Historical Society Library, the New York Public Library, the Duke University Library, the University of North Carolina Library, the University of South Carolina Library, and the State Library of Tennessee. To many others —notably Mrs. Mary Callaway Jones, historian-general of the United Daughters of the Confederacy; Mrs. Thomas Sloo, of New Orleans; Mrs. Julia R. Cleveland and Mrs. Felicia Cleveland Starr, of San Antonio; Mrs. Alice Brent, of Baltimore; Mrs. J. E. Hays, state historian of Georgia; Dr. William D. Hoyt, Jr., of Baltimore; Mr. T. R. Hay, of Locust Valley, New York; Dr. T. Harry Williams, of Louisiana State University; Dr. William D. McCain, of the Mississippi Department of Archives and History; Mrs. Marie B. Owen, of the Alabama Depart-

ment of Archives and History; Mr. G. B. Harrison,
Jr., of Baylor University; Mr. Hicklin P. Hunnicutt,
of Austin; and Mr. Daniel S. Ruggles, of Dallas—
who gave advice, furnished information, or loaned
family papers, I am profoundly grateful.

WILLIAM B. HESSELTINE

Madison, Wisconsin
November, 1949

Contents

[xi]

I.

Davis versus Lee: the Rivalry of Philosophy and Realism

THROUGH the perfervid propaganda of the Republican North, in the years during and after the War Against the States, there ran one continuous thread: the "leaders" of the South had misled the Southern people into a war for the defense of slavery. In 1880, William Cullen Bryant, sometime editor and erstwhile poet, lent his august name to *A Popular History of the United States*. At the beginning of the chapter on the war, the famed author revealed his profound belief that the South's leaders had been engaged in a vile conspiracy. "This volume has missed its aim," he confessed, "if it has not shown the central fact of the history of the United States to be, from the beginning of the century to the beginning of the slaveholders' rebellion, a determination of a class to get possession of the Government for its own purposes."

Bryant was, fifteen years after the war, only echoing the orthodox doctrine. Charles Sumner estimated that secession was the work of twenty men: Edward Everett lowered the estimate to ten. And John S. C.

Abbott, a popular historian who had already turned out a history of the French Revolution and a biography of Napoleon, produced, before the war was half over, a two-volume "history" which elaborated upon the theme that a handful of Southern "leaders" had conspired to overthrow democratic government, establish a monarchy in the South, and perpetuate a system of hereditary aristocracy. He made a point that only forty-two men formed the Confederacy's provisional government at Montgomery and "undertook to revolutionize a nation of thirty millions." In fact, said historian Abbott, "very great ability was displayed by the leaders of this conspiracy. They were men of thought, of wealth, and were long accustomed to the exercise of power. They were few in numbers, and could thus act with almost the energy of a single despotic mind." Carefully, the historian explained the nature of the South's leaders: "On their remote plantations, surrounded only by their colored menials, not one of whom could testify in any court of justice, they ruled with a despotic power which felt no restraint. They could torture, maim, kill at pleasure. Thus they have formed a character of arrogance and of ferocity, which must excite the amazement and execration of the civilized world. The evidence upon this point cannot be resisted by any honest mind."

Whatever the value of such statements as propaganda, they hardly constituted an accurate estimate of the leaders of the Southern Confederacy. Long years after Abbott's neurotic description and Bryant's suave repetition of wartime hysteria, another historian, casting a caustic eye upon the era, lumped Southern and Northern leaders together as "a blundering generation."

Harsh though the latter judgment may be, it probably came nearer the truth than the war-born allegation that the South's leaders were arrogant, ferocious despots united in a diabolic conspiracy. The South's leaders came from many walks of life, had a varied background, and possessed no single common characteristic. Certainly, as the internal history of the Confederacy testifies, they did not act with "a single despotic mind."

Had there been a *Who's Who in the Confederacy,* issued by some enterprising Richmond publisher for the edification of newspaper offices, bureau officials, and academy librarians, it might have contained perhaps a thousand names. Herded for ready reference into an alphabetic queue would have been cryptic sketches of the leading editors, the top ranks of the industrial hierarchy, the college professors, the tycoons of business, the authors of books, the inventors of gadgets, and even a few representatives of the upper echelons of the *Social Register.* But, for the most part, this imagined volume would have listed the high civil and military officials of the embattled Southland. There would have been President Jefferson Davis and his cabinet, the members of the provisional and permanent congresses, the judges of the courts, the governors of the states, and the wandering members of the diplomatic corps who pleaded the South's wavering cause before foreign thrones. And there would have been, too, the military men—from Brigadier General Daniel W. Adams, a graduate of the University of Virginia who, in his early forties, laid aside his Louisiana law practice to take up the sword, to Brigadier General William H. Young, another Virginia graduate who had been a member of the bar in San Antonio. Between these University of Virginia lawyers at the alphabetic extremes would have been the eight full generals with whom the Confederate army began, some three hundred other general officers, a score or more of naval commanders, and a squad or two of staff officers, bureau chiefs, and chaplains whose influence or strategic placement entitled them to listing among the Confederate leaders.

Such a list—had it ever been compiled—would have shown that the South's leaders had not all, by any means, come from "remote plantations" where they had exercised despotic sway over colored menials. Many—in fact, the overwhelming majority— had come from the lesser walks of life and had risen through merit or favoritism or luck to posts of power. Many of the leaders, too were military men to whom the national holocaust gave opportunity to display their talents for leadership. But, though no *Who's Who in the Confederacy* was ever compiled, the

[4]

record of these leaders, military and civil, was for-ever written in the history of the Lost Cause. The record of their deeds in the council hall and on the battlefield bore testimony to their statesmanship, their political acumen, their strategic insight, their tactical ability, and their gallant heroism. It told, as well, a story of partisan bickering, of gross incom-petence, and of predacious trickery. Perhaps, in the end, it showed that each generation of men is a blun-dering one.

But though the Confederacy's cause was lost on the battlefield, the Confederate leaders remained to face the problems of the postwar South. They who had led the Southern people were still, after Ap-pomattox, the leaders. Though what they had done, or had failed to do, may have contributed to the end, the leaders had not been discredited. In the last anal-ysis, the Confederacy had collapsed before the onslaughts of overwhelming military power; and the leaders—defeated but not conquered—emerged from the conflict as popular heroes who had gallantly waged a righteous war in a holy cause. In the popular mind, it was the leaders of the disaffected peace men and the Unionists who deserved opprobrium. Backed by popular acclaim and freighted with public respon-sibility, the Confederate leaders turned their talents, their virtues, and their capacities to the tasks of re-construction and rehabilitation.

From the beginning two obstacles confronted the

Confederate leaders who sought to beat their swords into plowshares. One was the economic and social ruin which the war had brought upon the Southern system. The other was the implacable hatred which their victorious enemies bore them. In December, 1863, Abraham Lincoln specifically excluded the high military and civil officers of the Confederacy from the amnesty he offered the Southern people; and in May, 1865, Andrew Johnson, reissuing his predecessor's proclamation, added wealthy Southerners to the excluded classes. The Fourteenth Amendment forbade Southern leaders to hold state or federal offices. Repeatedly Northern pundits demanded a blood sacrifice to expiate the South's sins. "If Toombs, Davis, Breckinridge and their fellow conspirators escape punishment," cried *Leslie's Illustrated Weekly,* "then indeed has 'Justice fled to brutish breasts and men have lost their reason.' " Only slowly, and then in piecemeal fashion, did Congress remove restrictions upon political activities and bestow amnesty upon selected Southern leaders. For long years the Grand Army of the Republic amicably met in encampment and passed fire-breathing resolutions against Confederate leaders, and Republican politicians "waved the bloody shirt" and cried havoc upon a thousand hustings against Davis and Lee and Stephens and Beauregard and Johnston and Hampton and Hill. "The magnanimity of our people is beyond question," boasted one vituperative writer in 1865, as he called for clemency to the "poor misguided masses." But "to *leaders* who precipitated us into four years of bloodshed and war, the severest punishment which law can give."

For a dozen years after Appomattox, the ruling party in the victorious North tried to impose a new body of leaders upon the Southern people. But neither the threat of reprisals nor the promise of patronage availed to entice Southerners to follow the guidance of imported carpetbaggers or native scalawags. Eventually, one by one, the Southern states were "redeemed" by their old leaders. The story of reconstruction is, in part, the story of the South's obstinate refusal to abandon the leaders who had guided the political and military destiny of the Confederate States of America.

The immediate reaction of the Southern leaders, as they faced the chaos of their social system, was a determination to rescue what they could from the wreck. Many—perhaps most—of them, faced with political disabilities, the threat of punishment, and the ruin of their hopes, gave thought to flight. Europe, Canada, and Latin America beckoned to them; and before the end of 1866 more than half a hundred left for temporary exile in Mexico, Canada, Cuba, South America, England or the Continent. At the same time a score left the South for the far West, the territories, or even the North. In the next fourteen years fifteen more left for foreign shores—five going to the Egyptian army and two to the Peruvian navy—and eighteen deserted the South for other parts of the United States. Most of those who left—like Governor Isham Harris of Tennessee, who spent a few months in Mexico—returned after longer or shorter periods in exile. Of more than six hundred leaders whose postwar careers left a record, only thirteen made permanent homes outside the United States. Except for Judah P. Benjamin, the most distinguished of the group, all had been military officers of the Confederacy. Another twenty-two, not counting senators and representatives, made their homes in Washington, D.C. Business opportunities took a bare handful of the Confederate leaders to New York and to California.

The great majority of the Confederacy's leading men, having cast a longing glance at foreign lands, urged their colleagues to remain in the South. Robert E. Lee's opinion was highly respected and widely quoted. "Virginia wants all their aid, all their support, and the presence of all her sons," declared the man who had drawn his sword in defense of his native state. "Our people should not leave," said Edmund Kirby-Smith. "Instead of seeking asylum abroad, their own destinies, and the triumph of the principles for which they fought, are in their own hands." In distant Texas, General James E. Harrison, who had tried to co-operate with the federal forces in effecting a peaceable disbanding of the western armies, proudly rejected the advice of friends that he leave the country. "I have a horror of running from my country like a criminal," he told his son. "I feel that I have done nothing wrong, or unworthy of a high-toned gentleman."

In part the Confederacy's leaders remained in the South because they still saw hope of rebuilding the South's economy and of restoring the states to their former place in the Union. General Harrison, busily preparing to "stand between the people of Texas and the Federal Army," believed that the "fundamental principles of government"—especially as they were "embraced in the Declaration of Rights"—could yet be peaceably established. General Robert E. Lee advised his soldiers to qualify themselves to vote and send "wise and patriotic men" to state legislatures and to Congress. Kirby-Smith urged Southerners to "seek by every possible means" the re-establishment of state governments. Eventually, he predicted, the military men would give way to civilians, and the South would unite with the Democratic party in the North to hold a balance of power and "secure the establishment of our rights, and the triumph of our principles."

Virginia's war governor, John Letcher, who had been a Unionist until the secession crisis forced his hand, came into the summer of 1865 with a politician's ebullient optimism. Federal troops had arrested him and then released him on parole. Before

[9]

returning to his Lexington home, "Honest John" visited Washington, where Andrew Johnson treated him courteously and "spoke in most liberal and conciliatory terms" about the South. "I am satisfied," reported Letcher, "he spoke his honest and sincere convictions, and I think it both politic and wise to meet him in the same spirit. If we do so I think we will find him our best friend."

In August Letcher made his way to the nearby Rockbridge Alum Springs. From the vantage ground of the famous watering place, the outlook seemed benign. "Everything in the county looks cheerful and inviting," he reported. The people were hard at work, the corn crop was the finest he had ever seen, and all the face of nature was kind. Moreover, he noted with satisfaction, "we have organized our County Court. . . . So many novel and difficult questions will now arise, that I anticipate a rich harvest to our profession. Indeed since the organization of the County Court, I have had many calls for advice in regard to matters that may form the basis of future suits of considerable magnitude. . . ."

But one thing gave Letcher a moment's pause—the Negro. "The sudden emancipation of the slaves embarrasses many of our largest farmers very seriously." Many slaves had gone off, and those who remained were indisposed to work But even here he was an optimist, counseling patience, making the best

[10]

of the situation, and looking forward hopefully to the future.

In the first weeks after Appomattox others besides Letcher looked at Southern society—especially at President Johnson's plans and at the Negro problem —and came away with varying answers. So far as Johnson's program was concerned, there were many who agreed with Letcher that the best policy was to work with the president. But Texas' General Harrison found Johnson's "system" an "extreme leveling one—uprooting the very foundations of our present and long established organism." The general, however, advised against political resistance and counseled only that Southerners accommodate themselves to the change. From Canada, Beverly Tucker, eventually to be a bishop, announced his intention to avoid a society in transition. "A despotism I *might* stand, but the Dominion of a *vulgar* despot— Never!" But from Canada, too, another voice from a clerical family put a different slant on the problems of society. The Reverend General William Nelson Pendleton, who soon would have Robert E. Lee as senior warden of his parish, read his daughter's observation from Canada that Northern newspapers were becoming "very earnest" about the impoverished condition of the South and "the absolute necessity of letting the people alone." Shrewdly she predicted that "Northern financiers will ere long take the alarm also, and

—out of sheer selfishness, the consciousness that Southern productiveness is the necessary basis of Northern wealth—will influence the law-makers and tax-voters to something more of justice to Southern property holders."

But whether hope sprang from Johnson's leniency or from Yankee acquisitiveness or whether despair reigned over threatened social upheavals, all the Southern leaders faced the problem of the ex-slaves. General Harrison was sorry for them, for want, poverty, buffetings, "famine, wretchedness and despair" would overtake them. "I want to take care of, and provide for mine if they will stay, behave themselves and work." When the Union general Gordon Granger arrived in Galveston, Harrison explained the situation; and Granger promptly announced that he would "not for one moment tolerate their leaving or vagabonding around the army." Harrison sent word to "his" Negroes to stay home until he could explain "everything" to them. "Poor miserable creatures," he sighed, "I don't know what is to become of them."

A Virginia colonel, however, believed that he could guess the Negro's future. As the Johnsonian government began to organize in the Old Dominion, he advised his banker that under Johnson's policy "we may by prudent legislation at home recover all we have lost—save slavery and even that will come again under another name." The Yankees, he went on to explain, needed cotton and a Southern market; and to get them they "would if they could kidnap and enslave angels from heaven." Stringent apprenticeship laws, he thought, would keep the country from supporting four million paupers and vagrants. But even that, he admitted finally, would not long forestall the social revolution. "Do what we may," he grieved, "the proud old race of country-gentlemen must disappear with the present generation—to be followed by a population of petty farmers and 'canaille.' "

Perhaps the most-discussed public statement of a high-placed Confederate in the first months after the war's end came from Postmaster General John H. Reagan. Captured with part of the Confederacy's records, Reagan went with other Confederate officials to Fort Warren prison. From his cell, Reagan surveyed the state of the South; and on the day before Johnson issued an amnesty proclamation and began to restore civil governments in the Southern states, the Confederate addressed an open letter to the president. In persuasive tones, Reagan pleaded for a humane and merciful policy rather than one "harsh, relentless and vindictive." There was, he declared, no need to fear revolt in the South; and a regime of punishment and confiscations would perpetuate hatred, reduce productiveness, and feed the fear of future revolts.

Pleased with Johnson's program, which seemed a reflection of his own ideas, Reagan turned to advising

[13]

the people of Texas how to escape military government and Negro suffrage. Still in prison, on August 11, the Confederate postmaster general admitted that his advice ran counter to all Southern education, tradition, and prejudices. Nevertheless, he told them, they were a conquered people, and they would have to submit to their victors. Resistance would not only prolong military government but might indeed lead to general military despotism. Texans should recognize the supreme authority of the United States, recognize the abolition of slavery, "and assent to great pecuniary sacrifices, momentous changes in your social and industrial system, and a surrender of your opinions." Specifically, he proposed to avoid Negro suffrage and prevent the Negroes from "becoming an element of political agitation and strife and danger" by according Negroes full legal equality, permitting them to testify in courts, and—finally—by fixing intellectual, moral, and property qualifications for all voters, black or white.

Whatever may have been said for Reagan's point of view—and he contended that both Alexander H. Stephens and Wade Hampton, as well as Massachusetts' Senator Henry Wilson, Secretary of State William H. Seward, Attorney General James Speed, and President Johnson endorsed it—the people of Texas were made of less pliable material. They rejected his advice, denounced him for subservience to the North, and excoriated him on political stumps in the futile campaigns of the first postwar summer.

Throughout that summer, as Southerners organized governments under Johnson's proclamations and Northern Radicals fumed in frustration as they waited for Congress to convene, there were other Southern leaders who, finding no hope in reconciliation through economics or politics, turned to religion. General Pendleton, returning to his pastorate, and rejecting his daughter's economic determinism, turned his thoughts to Heaven. Probably defeat was divine punishment for having been "idolators in our estimate of Virginia," and now that "we must be content to live without a country" the people could have their "hearts engrossed with that better land where no sin enters, and where peace and charity prevail forever." Jesus, the apostles, and the martyrs had been sustained as they lived under foreign domination! General James E. Harrison, too, advised his people to cultivate "the more refining influences of our nature and above all seek a refuge in the Savior, attend all the means of grace, preserve a pious and dignified deportment, trust and serve God, and eventually all will be well." But even religion was not a solace to Robert Louis Dabney, professor in the Union Theological Seminary who had been chaplain and chief of staff to the crusading Presbyterian, Stonewall Jackson. He believed that the only chance of preserving the "true Christianity of the South" was to transplant it to another clime. Eagerly he began a correspondence with General Jubal A. Early and the geographer Matthew Fontaine Maury to find an earthly home where he could bring up his children under moral influences.

Thus, amid a confusion of tongues, the Confederate leaders faced the future. And however much of resignation and despair might creep into their speech, the men who had led the Confederacy were still the leaders of the Southern people. What they would do to bring order out of economic chaos, to re-create a political system, to reorganize and reorient Southern culture would, in the years to come, profoundly affect both the South and the reunited nation.

Only a handful of the leading Confederates failed to make their mark in the postwar years. A few of the elder statesmen and the older soldiers folded their hands and passed into oblivion. Some of them died, of heartbreak, wounds, and disease, within a few months after Appomattox. But of 656 prominent Confederates who lived long enough to make postwar readjustments, only 71 failed to recover a substantial portion of the position and prestige they had enjoyed at the Confederacy's peak. The forgotten 71 left no records which inquisitive historians of a later day could evaluate.

The remaining 585 Confederate leaders who made

their contributions to the new nation had indeed been prominent in the Confederacy. They had held a total of 622 offices in the four years of the South's struggle for nationhood. Three hundred and forty-two had been military leaders, and 273 had held important posts as civilians.

Among the 342 military officers were 225 brigadier generals, 81 general officers of higher rank, 25 naval officers, 2 field officers, and 9 chaplains who, as chiefs of staff (like Robert Louis Dabney) or by virtue of their personal influence, had sat in the councils of the great. The civilians included President Davis, Vice-President Stephens, the cabinet, and other executives (a total of 23), 7 judges, 173 representatives and 28 senators, 22 governors, 19 other state officials, 7 diplomats, and an Indian agent. Of course, there were duplications between the lists: 27 of the leading men had held two or even three high-ranking positions. Two brigadier generals were also governors, one brigadier was also a senator, and 7 brigadiers and 2 major generals served in the Confederate House of Representatives. Two generals were executives of bureaus; 2 were, in addition to their military rank, both congressmen and governors; and one brigadier general was also a naval officer. Civilians, too, held several posts. Two were both congressmen and diplomats; 2 were both congressmen and judges; 3 were congressmen and bureau chiefs; 7 were both representatives and senators; one was a bureau administrative officer who served the Confederacy abroad. The 585 leaders came into the New South with a rich background of experience.

They had represented the states of the South in rough proportion to their respective populations. Virginia, however, with 17.8 per cent of the Confederacy's free population—more than a third of whom were in the disaffected mountain counties—furnished 101, or 27.3 per cent of the 585. The disproportion may have confirmed the oft expressed charge that Virginians dominated the army and the government of the Confederate states. The charge probably came most frequently from Georgia, which, although it had practically the same population and far less disaffection, filled slightly less than 11 per cent of the higher offices. Almost 12 per cent of the South's leaders came from outside the Confederacy—from Kentucky, Missouri, Maryland, and the territories—while 10 of the total number were non-Southern in origin and prewar residence.

In addition to experience, the great majority of this group of leaders had had the advantages of an education. Only 26 of the 585 had had little or no formal schooling. On the other hand, among the others, 32 had attended academies before the war— 8 in the North and 24 in the South; 102 had gone to college—8 in the North, and 94 in the South; and 165 had gone to universities—118 of them to Southern schools. Among those who had gone to Northern universities, 16 had spent some time at Harvard, 13 at Yale, 12 at Princeton, and 3 at Brown. Graduates or former cadets of West Point numbered 120, while 19 had received military training in Southern military schools. There were 6 who had been educated abroad, 6 who had received private instruction, and 7 who had attended theological seminaries. Still others had attended law schools, medical colleges, teacher-training institutes, or the naval academy at Annapolis.

In the years before the war, these men had followed a variety of trades and professions. The majority, as befitted a land where the law was the natural steppingstone to public office, were lawyers. There were 304 practicing lawyers in the group. Next in number were the 145 officers of the United States army and navy—104 of whom had been in active service in 1861. Planters or farmers added 134—far outnumbering the 37 educators, the 27 merchants, and the 25 editors who made up the next largest economic groups. Before the war, too, 18 of the Confederate leaders had been civil engineers, and 16 had been connected with railroads. There were 13 in banks—ranging from tellers to presidents—and 14 were in the ministry—ranging from curates to bishops. There were 10 physicians, 2 steamship captains, and 2 building contractors. One was a brickmason, one a tailor, and one a tavern keeper. Of the whole group, 166 had had political prominence—at least they had held office beyond the courthouse hierarchy of their home counties.

At the close of the war, despite their years of education and experience, the majority of the Confederacy's leaders were men between thirty and fifty years of age. A reticent group of 65 men never revealed their age, but the remaining 520 showed no such feminine reserve. Among them, 26 were under thirty when Lee's surrender checked their careers, another 136 were in their thirties, and 191 were between forty and fifty years old. A group of 122 were above fifty but had not yet reached sixty, 45 were between sixty and sixty-nine, and 4 were over seventy. In general, the military men were younger than their civilian colleagues. More than three fourths of the general officers, for example, were under fifty in 1865, while one half of the congressmen had passed the half-century mark.

The age of the leaders made it reasonably certain that they would live long enough to impress themselves upon a newer generation of Southerners. By 1890, after the trials of reconstruction and the years of reorganization, 50 per cent of the Confederacy's leaders were still alive. Within the first five years after Appomattox 41 leaders died; in the next decade 101 passed away. But although 281 were living in 1890, only 134 survived the century. Another decade, however, saw but 41 still alive, and only 2 leaders lived beyond the end of World War I.

In the course of the years between the siege of Petersburg and the battle of the Argonne, the Confederate leaders made many adjustments to a changing world. In the beginning their most pressing problem was economic: the professional soldiers among them must find entirely new vocations; and even among those who did not have to seek new careers, few indeed—military officers or civilians—could immediately return to their prewar trades. For the overwhelming majority, peace meant months—and sometimes years—of search for new means of making a living.

Eventually—although in many cases after much trial and error—the Confederate leaders found economic outlets for their talents. For some, their old employments had no longer either charm or emolument. The lawyers, for example, decreased in numbers from 304 before the war to 292 after the conflict—and, of course, not all of these were the same men. Farmers and planters, however, increased in number—from 134 to 193—partly, at least, through the sheer need for food. The teaching profession also profited from new recruits—its members rising from 37 to 66 in number. The merchants among the leading group grew from 27 to 39, the editors rose from 25 to 29, and the clergymen increased their number from 14 to 27; the doctors, however, declined from 10 to 6. But the greatest proportionate increase took place in banking, railroading, and industry. Before the war, 13 of the leaders had been employed in banks; after it 23 were so employed. There had been 16 ante-bellum railroad men among the leading group; 73 found positions on postwar railroads. Mining and industry claimed a scant 14 in 1860, but 34 leaders became prominent industrialists in the New South.

In addition, in the postwar years, new occupational groups appeared. Some 30 of the leaders, capitalizing on their prestige, became chronic government job-holders, picking the poor crumbs of patronage which Southern Democrats might dispense. Another 25 became insurance agents, wheedling their old companions-in-arms to buy policies or to borrow money at usurious rates. A dozen turned professional lecturers or writers, distilling a heady oratory or a flamboyant style from their battle experiences. Ten became officers in foreign armies and navies, 3 were police chiefs, 2 were express agents, and 2 were cattle dealers.

The group of Confederate leaders who had the greatest adjustment to make were those—104 in number—who were officers of the United States army and navy in 1861. Only one—General Joseph Wheeler—returned eventually to his original profession in the United States, though a half-dozen or more continued their military career under alien flags. The others found other employment: 44 as farmers, 20 as educators, 14 as merchants, 13 as insurance agents, 14 as civil engineers, 10 as lawyers, 9 as government job-holders, 3 as steamship captains, 3 as bankers, 2 as station agents, and one each as railroad superintendent, express agent, and chief of police.

However diverse their economic activities, the Confederate leaders in the postwar years gave general adherence to the Democratic party. Only 22 at one time or another joined the Republicans, and only 2 were Populists. As soon as possible, most of the politicians among the Confederacy's leaders offered themselves to the voters. Within a decade 104 held state offices, 18 sat in state constitutional conventions, 2 served on code-revision commissions, and 24 held county jobs. Between 1875 and 1885, a decade marked by the final "redemption" of the states from carpetbag and Negro rule, 128 were state officials, 31 were members of constitutional conventions, 4 helped to revise codes, and 23 were ensconced in county courthouses. Advancing age and death—but probably never resignations—reduced the number of state officeholders between 1885 and 1895 to 65, and in the next ten-year period to 17. But in 1905 still 3 of the group were state officers.

The variety of local posts which these veteran leaders filled ran the full gamut of officialdom. Among the local officers 6 Confederate leaders were county judges; 5 were mayors; 4 were sheriffs; 3 each were police chiefs and city attorneys; and 2 each were county-court clerks, tax collectors, and commissioners of public works. One was a crier in a city court, one a surveyor, one a city councilman, and one a city superintendent of schools.

In the states, the Confederate leaders served in equally varied capacities. They numbered 30 governors, 29 state senators, and 44 assemblymen; 35 were judges of lower courts and 14 of supreme courts; 12 were chief justices of their states. Railroad commissions gave employment to 8 Confederate leaders; 7 were attorney generals; 5 were superintendents of state prisons; 4 were state engineers; 3 were commissioners of immigration. Some among them served as lieutenant governors, secretaries of state, treasurers, comptrollers and auditors, and superintendents of education. They were councilors of state, chancellors, and state solicitors. They were commissioners for the relief of the destitute, for public works, for insurance, for "statistics and history." One was a superintendent of buildings and grounds, one directed a state bureau of agriculture, one was superintendent of a deaf-and-dumb asylum, and one was commander of the Chesapeake Bay oyster patrol.

But it was not only in cities, counties, and states that the ex-Confederate leaders served in public office. They held an almost equally great assortment of posts, elective or appointive, in the national government. In Congress there were 45 representatives and 28 senators—the "rebel brigadiers," whose verbal adherence to ancient Southern principles sometimes outraged the representatives of Northern constituencies—and there was one clerk of the House, one doorkeeper, and one secretary of the Senate who had been prominent in the Confederacy. One Confederate leader became a justice of the Supreme Court; one, secretary of the interior; and one, attorney general. Twenty-two posts representing the United States in dealing with foreign affairs went to the ex-Confederate leaders—11 as ministers, 3 as consuls general, 5 as consuls, 2 on boards of international arbitration, and one as a Cuban peace commissioner. Indian affairs and the land office furnished them 13 posts; 7 were postmasters; 5 were United States marshals. Two were superintendents of the New Orleans mint; 3 surveyors or collectors of ports. Federal commissions, too, used the talents of the Confederacy's onetime leaders: one served on the Interstate Commerce Commission, one on the Civil Service Commission, 2 on the Tariff Commission, and 4 on a railroad commission. And there were even a few whose Confederate experiences were the direct cause of their federal appointment: the War Department employed 4 Confederates to collect and edit Confederate records, and 3 Confederates served on the park commissions for the Antietam, Vicksburg, and Gettysburg national parks.

Their successful economic rehabilitation and political restoration bore tribute both to the aggressiveness and to the resiliency of the Confederacy's sometime leading men. The fact that they remained in the South—and that of the few who fled, in panic or despair, the majority came back—gave testimony both to the willingness of the Southern people to continue to follow and even to reward them, and to the eventual willingness of the victorious federal government to tolerate them. Yet their careers provided no evidence that the ex-Confederates spoke with a single, unifying voice on the problems and direction of the New South.

The facts were quite the opposite. The leading spirits of the Confederacy had never been united in policy or program. In the secession crisis they had spoken with confused tongues: some had favored secession because they were ardent Southern nationalists, some because they believed a temporary separation would give them a better vantage ground for bargaining and compromise with the North; others were Unionists or "co-operationists" who fought secession and only "went along with the section" when they were overwhelmed. Once the Confederate States of America began to function as an organized government, the old divisions reappeared. Proponents of states' rights battled against Jefferson Davis' nationalizing tendencies, Unionists favored peaceful adjustments with the North, and romantic individualists became disgruntled with conscription and wartime regimentation. Confusion of counsel marked the days of the Confederacy and divided the South's leaders in the postwar years.

Fundamentally the divisions of the postwar decades had roots which ran deep into the ante-bellum period. Their manifestations, however, took the form of controversy over the adjustments which the South should make to the new order. In a sense, it was a question of whether Appomattox had surrendered the Southern cause or only Lee's armies. At opposite poles on this basic question stood the two men who were first in the Confederacy—President Jefferson Davis, the political leader, and General Robert Edward Lee, commander of the Southern armies.

Symbolic of the basic division between Davis and Lee were their first acts after Appomattox. Sorrowfully Lee bade farewell to his soldiers and returned to his family, while Davis, hoping still to rally the remnants of the South's forces, fled into the deep South. Captured and carried to Fortress Monroe, chained in his cell, charged with conspiring to murder prisoners and to assassinate Lincoln, and indicted for treason against the United States, Davis never surrendered, never confessed to wrongdoing or to bad judgment, and never advised Southerners to wear the yokes of their Yankee conquerors. The proud Lee, turning his energies, his talents, and his prestige to building a New South, and the defiant Davis, seeking

[27]

constantly to justify and perpetuate the Old South, became the embodied symbols of the basic conflicts in Southern life. Near to them—each in his own fashion—gathered the erstwhile leaders of the Southern Confederacy.

Robert E. Lee spent the last five years of his life giving the Southern people a practical demonstration of submission to their conquerors. He abhorred the idea of abandoning the country: "I prefer," he stated repeatedly, "to struggle for its restoration and share its fate, rather than give up all as lost." Recognizing his own position in the hearts of Southerners, the commander of the Confederate armies felt a heavy responsibility to conduct himself becomingly. "Obedience to lawful authority is the foundation of manly character," declared the man who had once described "duty" as the noblest word in the English language. Duty now, in his opinion, called for "everyone to unite in the restoration of the country and the re-establishment of peace and harmony." So far as the greatest Confederate soldier was concerned, the war was at an end, the Southern states had laid down their arms, and "the questions at issue between them and the Northern States" had been decided.

With such opinions, Lee counseled Southerners to engage in politics and accept the consequences of defeat. He, himself, set an example by applying for pardon from Andrew Johnson, and he advised others to do so. Since he was never pardoned, he carefully refrained from public statements on political issues; but his private counsel, frequently given, advised Southerners to participate actively. When approached by ardent Democrats with a proposition that he run for governor, he refused because his candidacy would be used by Northerners to injure the people of Virginia.

On the burning question of the Negro and Negro suffrage, Marse Robert counseled moderation. Summoned before the Joint Committee on Reconstruction, he told the amazed Radicals that the Negroes were quiet and orderly, that the whites were kind to them, that the farmers preferred their old servants as workers, and that the people wanted the blacks educated because it would be better for both races. But, in complete honesty, he informed the committee, "I do not think that the black man is as capable of acquiring knowledge as the white man." Some Negroes were, of course, "more apt" than others, and Lee had had slaves of his own "who learned to read and write very well." Even so, he advised conservative men to vote for a Virginia constitution granting Negro suffrage. Conservatives might then gain control of the state, and improve the constitution as opportunity offered.

But if Lee would not make a public statement on political affairs, he would participate actively in economic advancement. In April, 1869, he co-operated with the people of Rockbridge and adjacent counties in an effort to induce the Baltimore and Ohio Railroad to extend its lines to Lexington, Virginia. Heading a delegation from Virginia's Valley counties, Lee journeyed to Baltimore to present the isolated region's case to the city's council and businessmen. The councilmen listened with interest, held a public reception for the Confederate hero and promised the Valley its road. In August of the following year, less than two months before his death, Lee accepted—at a salary of $5,000 a year—the chairmanship of the Valley group of subscribers to the road.

En route from his Baltimore ovation, Lee stopped in Washington to call, by invitation, on President Ulysses S. Grant. The commanders of the opposing armies had not met since Appomattox, and their personalities had little in common. Grant was chatty, informal, given to pleasantries in conversation. The president of Washington College was a dignified gentleman of the old school. With less business to transact than when they had met at McLean's house, the two men were both uncomfortable during the brief interview in the White House. Yet the meeting was a symbolic ratification of Appomattox: General Lee had surrendered far more than the Army of Northern Virginia.

The surrender had involved no emotional change. "Did you ever feel resentment toward the North?" asked a friend on one occasion. Solemnly Lee replied: "I believe I may say, looking into my own heart, and speaking as in the presence of God, that I have never known one moment of bitterness or resentment." When a student spoke harshly about the North, President Lee admonished him by talking about the Union. And once the general took pains to recall that he had been opposed to secession and to war, and in favor of the Constitution and the Union "established by our forefathers." No one, he added, "is more in favor of that Constitution and that Union."

Yet Lee had no regrets for his own course and no feeling of wrongdoing. He took pride in the South, in the heroism of its people, and in the bravery of his soldiers. To a student who wanted to "make up for time lost in the army" the old commander insisted, "However long you live, and whatever you accomplish, you will find that the time you spent in the Confederate army was the most profitably spent portion of your life." Prizing his own experiences, Lee planned to write his memoirs. Hardly had the soldiers gotten home—in fact, the last Confederate army had not even surrendered—when Lee wrote his subordinates asking for reports and documents. Officers sent him materials, and Lee engaged many of them in a general correspondence about military affairs. He urged James A. Longstreet, Wade Hampton, and others to write. Every officer, he thought, should do so. "It is the only way in which we may hope that fragments of truth will reach posterity."

But the general never wrote his memoirs. His

financial situation never permitted him the leisure time for literary composition. When the war closed, Lee's property was gone, and he sought a means of earning a livelihood. Business positions—which would capitalize on his name—he rejected. He turned down a position at the University of the South because it was a church school and one at the University of Virginia because it was a state school. But Washington College at Lexington, Virginia, was nominally independent of Presbyterian control, and Lee accepted its presidency—at a salary of $1,500 and 15 per cent of the students' tuition fees.

"It is particularly incumbent upon those charged with the instruction of the young to set them an example of submission to authority," said Lee to the trustees as he accepted the presidency. "The proper education" of Southern youth, he believed, would produce the greatest benefits and would be the most efficacious means of promoting the prosperity of the South. He was determined, he explained, "to educate Southern youth into a spirt of loyalty to the new conditions and the transformation of the social fabric which had resulted from the war, and only through a peaceful obedience to which could the future peace and harmony of the country be restored."

Completely lacking any understanding of Lee's attitude, *Harper's Weekly* greeted the announcement of Lee's acceptance of the presidency by comparing Lee to Benedict Arnold: "Truth, rhetoric, and patriotism are equally cheap, it seems, at Washington College." The New York *Independent,* another hate-mongering Radical organ, denounced Lee as "the bloodiest and guiltiest traitor in all the South." But within a few years understanding dawned upon the North, and the New York *Herald* prophesied that Lee would "make as great an impression on our old fogy schools" as he had upon the North's old-fogy military commanders.

Within the next five years, President Lee gave a practical demonstration, at Washington College, of his doctrine of political, economic, and educational submission. The college over which he took control had forty students and four professors. Its buildings had been ransacked by Hunter's raid, its apparatus destroyed, and its minuscule library scattered. Its endowment, accumulating since George Washington's initial gift, was unproductive. Yet before his death in 1870, Lee saw the student body increase to nearly five hundred students, most of whom were veterans of the Confederate armies; the faculty increase to twenty-one; and his own salary grow to nearly $5,000 a year. He restored the buildings, improved the grounds, and built a chapel. The old endowment began to bring in a revenue, and new donors added substantially to the funds.

But the most startling change at Washington College came in the curriculum. Taking over an old-style classical college whose emphasis had been on Greek,

Latin, and moral philosophy, Lee presided over the institution as it added courses in engineering, law, commerce, agriculture, modern languages (including Spanish), and even journalism. The object of the scientific program, Lee explained to the trustees, "is to provide the facilities required by the large class of our young men who, looking to early entrance into practical pursuits of life, need a more direct training to this end." The new program would not only "call forth the genius and energies of our people" but also "develop the resources and promote the interests" of the South. Clearly this was not, as the Chicago *Tribune* had declared it to be, "a school run principally for the propagation of hatred to the Union."

Closely combined with this interest in scientific and practical education was Lee's continuing interest in religion. Personally devout, he made every effort to instill religious principles in the students of Washington College. He used the first funds collected to build a college chapel, placing it in front of the row of older college buildings. He daily attended exercises in the building. He supported a Y.M.C.A. at the college. He advised students about their religious life and once told a local minister, "I dread the thought of any student going away from the College without becoming a sincere Christian." Under his inspiration the college adopted the honor system. In his disciplinary activities—always an important presidential chore in his day—he relied on moral appeals. The greatest mistake of his life, he declared, had been in taking a military education. "Self controlled obedience to constituted authority"—the self-control resting on religious sanctions—was his ideal.

With such an ideal, with scientific progress and religious faith going hand in hand, Lee became the embodiment of the spirit of the New South. It was a South which, following Lee's example, would abandon its past, forsake its rural folkways, and discard the romantic notions and the constitutional theories which had led to disastrous defeat—to build a new society on a Northern model.

But while Lee, carrying out the terms of Appomattox to their logical conclusion, was laying the theoretical bases for the New South, Jefferson Davis, political leader who had once considered himself the heir of John C. Calhoun, was seeking to preserve the ideals, the ideology, and the social structure of the Old South. Jefferson Davis had fled, and he had been captured. But he never surrendered.

For almost a quarter of a century after Appomattox, Jefferson Davis held aloft the Confederate flag. For the first two years he was a prisoner in Fortress Monroe, awaiting trial—first on charges of having conspired with the assassins of Lincoln, and then under indictment for treason. Released on bail in 1867, he journeyed to Canada and Europe before finally returning to Mississippi. In 1871 he became president of the Carolina Life Insurance Company of Memphis and managed the affairs of the struggling, inadequately financed company until it failed in 1874. Another trip to England followed, and for a couple of years Davis hoped to launch a steamship company to ply between New Orleans and South America. But that, too, failed; and by 1877 Davis had settled to the life of a Mississippi planter, eking out an income by writing articles for Northern magazines and by lecturing. Financially, his *Rise and Fall of the Confederate Government,* published in 1881, was a failure.

From the beginning Davis bore the brunt of Northern hatred. *Harper's Weekly* and other bloodthirsty sheets called for his execution. The New York *Times* denounced him as the "prime mover in the rebellion" and declared that an "endeavor to save him from retributive justice is to outrage every enlightened sentiment, every unperverted instinct." And Andrew Johnson called for "halter and gallows" for Davis and all the "conscious, intelligent, leading traitors." Under such demands, the captured Davis was put in irons until returning public sanity demanded their removal.

Davis' harsh imprisonment brought its rewards. At the time he was captured he had lost all the confidence of the Southern people. The mounting opposition to his administration, the growing disillusionment with the Confederacy's hopes, the declining morale, the irritating squabbles with weary and despairing commanders had combined to make Davis the symbol of Confederate frustration. But his long imprisonment won him sympathy; the beginnings of reconstruction and the quarrel between Johnson and the Radicals diverted attention from him; and the absurdity of the charge that he had plotted with Lincoln's murderer won him support. When he was released from prison, ex-Postmaster General Reagan could truthfully tell him that "the great mass of our people regard you as suffering in your own person for and on account of them." Inadvertently, the Northern government had restored Davis to the affections of the Southern people.

Never again did Davis lose his place as the beloved leader of the Lost Cause. He capitalized upon his martyrdom as Charles Sumner had once done. Quickly he assumed the role that Northern stupidity had thrust upon him: "The consolation which I derived from the intense malignity shown to me by the enemy was in the hope that their hate would, by concentration on me, be the means of relieving my countrymen." He had become victim instead of villain, and he longed for the day when he could "behold retributive justice upon the knaves now flourishing."

Carl Schurz, who had never lost an opportunity to make political capital from war-born hatreds, complained that Davis was a sour man who "stimulated the brooding over the past disappointments rather than cheerful contemplation of new opportunities." But Davis had only contempt for "men who once led in Southern movements" who were "degrading themselves, gaining power and place." Instead of following their example he urged Southerners to "preserve the traditions of our Fathers, and to keep in honorable remembrance the deeds of our Brothers."

For himself, the Confederate president devoted his efforts to elaborating the doctrine of states' rights and the cause of constitutional government. On the burning issue of the Negro he had little to say—and that little bore no animosity toward the ex-slave. Before the war, Jefferson and his brother Joseph had been distinguished for their efforts to reform the organization of plantation life and to improve the living conditions of their slaves. From his prison cell Davis wrote his wife about his real distress over the fate of the black man. "The Negro is unquestionably to be at last the victim," he prophesied, "because when brought into conflict, the inferior race must be overborne." He hoped, however, that the conflict might be deferred and "a part of the kind relations heretofore existing between the races when a lifelong common interest united them" might be preserved. He believed, too, that the "operation of the ordinary laws governing the relation of labor to capital" would eventually correct the evils done by Radical meddling. Certainly, in his defense of the South, Davis was prepared to battle against the Northern doctrine that the Confederacy was a conspiracy for the perpetuation of slavery.

The cause of the Confederacy, as Davis reiterated· in speech after speech, in hundreds of private letters, in magazine articles, and in his *Rise and Fall of the Confederate Government,* was the cause of constitutional liberty. The states were sovereign, and secession was a sovereign right. The war showed secession to be impractical; it did not prove it wrong. "Until I can be convinced that we were rebels, traitors, and warring against the compact of our Fathers," he told General Jubal A. Early, "it will not be possible for me to join the throng who hurrah for the pillagers and houseburners who invaded our homes." Once he addressed the Mississippi legislature, explaining that he had never applied for pardon because repentance must precede pardon, "and I have not repented." The Southerners had fought to maintain their birthright of sovereignty, freedom, and independence. "They were right and will yet be found right."

Until his death in December, 1889, Jefferson Davis reiterated the theme that the states had the constitutional right to secede. Even after his death, the *North American Review* published his last article on "The Doctrine of States Rights." Essentially, said Davis, the doctrine was not that of a section but that "of a minority, seeking the protection of State sovereignty from the real or supposed aggression of a usurping minority." Here, as in his other writings,

Davis had not grown beyond the point which Calhoun reached. But he had, through the years, clarified his constitutional thinking, elaborated and strengthened the arguments of Southerners of 1861, and convinced himself again of his own rectitude. He had, moreover, won the right to be classed among the South's leading political philosophers. If he was not the greatest among them, he had clear title to be considered the last.

Around Davis and the standard he upheld, more and more Southerners gathered. Confederate leaders who could not follow the advice of Lee—men who would not concede that the issues had been settled on the battlefield—rallied to Davis' support. Lieutenant General Jubal A. Early, who fled to Mexico and then to Canada after the war but later returned to his Lynchburg, Virginia, law practice, organizer and first president of the Southern Historical Society and sometime head of the Louisiana Lottery, was Davis' constant correspondent and supporter. John William Jones, chaplain of Virginia troops, Baptist minister, and secretary of the Southern Historical Society, eagerly encouraged Davis in his writing and begged the Confederate president to go on a lecture tour for the society. Georgia's Professor William M. Browne, English-born editor who had been assistant secretary of state, wrote Davis that it disgusted him to see the "spread of apostacy" among "our own people." Contemptuously he repeated the apostate slogans: " 'We must not offend our friends at the North,' 'The war is over,' 'The sooner we forget it the better,' 'We need their money,' 'It is bad policy to justify what we did.'" Look at William Mahone, invited Browne, as he added, "I will visit you this summer [1882] and renew and strengthen my faith by converse with its greatest, and most earnest apostle."

And other Southerners renewed and strengthened their faith at Davis' feet. In his last years, the Confederate president gained a degree of popularity he had never known in the Confederate States of America. As Lee became the symbol of the Lost Cause, Jefferson Davis became the living reminder that the cause of the Confederacy, of states' rights, of liberty under the constitution, of the protection of minorities against national centralization lived on. Between the Old South, which was, in its way, the old Federal Union, and the New South, which subscribed to the concepts and practices of the new nation—between, in fact, the traditions of Robert E. Lee and those of Jefferson Davis—there was a continuing conflict.

It was a conflict with many manifestations. Men divided along the lines of Davis and Lee in religion, in education, in politics, and in economics. Eventually, in both the South and the nation as a whole, a working compromise was found between the antagonistic ideologies; but the struggle itself left a long legacy of conflict in the life of the South.

II.

Clashing Counselors in Church
and School

THE PROBLEMS and confusions of the postwar leaders of the defunct Confederacy, the
dichotomy of ideology between those who would preserve the Old South and those who would put hands
to the plow of the New South without a backward
glance, the tuggings of nostalgia and the urgings of
hope were nowhere better illustrated than in the
careers of those Confederate leaders who preached
in the pulpits or taught in the schools. Religious and
educational institutions had furnished a fair quota of
leaders to the Confederacy; they received more than
a fair proportion of the leaders after the war. Perhaps it was economic pressure and the availability
of jobs in the schools that led many Southern leaders
to turn to education; perhaps it was a sense of responsibility for the youth whom they had led in battle
that caused generals to change from plumed hats to
mortarboards. Whatever the motive, many a leader
of the Confederacy assumed the role of priest or
pedagogue—and sometimes both—in the days after
Appomattox.

Religion had played an important role in shaping the thought processes of the Old South. At a time when Unitarianism, Spiritualism, and Mormonism were rising in the ante-bellum North, the religious scene in the South was showing an increasing tendency toward theological and social conservatism. Southern ministers became defenders of slavery and vigorous opponents of the heterodox "isms" of Yankeedom. The sectional split of national denominations furnished ecclesiastical precedents for secession. It was not without significance that the Reverend Brigadier General William Nelson Pendleton named the guns of his battery for Matthew, Mark, Luke, and John— or that he regarded "abolitionism as one of the specious forms of atheism."

Throughout the war, as many observers noted, a religious revival raged with full emotional intensity in the ranks of the Confederate army. The leaders of the army, like Lee and Jackson, were pious, prayerful men, setting an example to officers and soldiers alike —such a profane agnostic as Jubal A. Early being a conspicuous exception. The romantic concept of the Christian knight inspired the Confederacy's leaders. Stonewall Jackson prayed in battle and hesitated to march on the Sabbath. Lieutenant General A. P. Stewart won the sobriquet "Old Straight," and news of the fall of Petersburg reached President Jefferson Davis in church.

Fourteen of the 585 most prominent leaders of

the Confederacy were ordained ministers before the Civil War; 27 of the leaders were active clergymen in the postwar years. Some of the additions were wartime converts; others sought ordination only after postwar conditions had turned their thoughts to religious matters. All of them remained in the South and gave their attention to religious work among the Southern people. If the effectiveness of their ministry can be gauged from the increase in the membership of their churches, the ex-Confederates were more successful in building the Kingdom of Heaven than they had been in establishing the Confederate States of America.

Among the Presbyterians, such leading Confederates as Benjamin Morgan Palmer and Moses Drury Hoge were conspicuous as builders of the denomination. New Orleans' Palmer had been commissioner of the Presbyterians to the Army of Tennessee, chaplain general of the armies of the Southwest, and moderator of the Presbyterian Church in the Confederate States of America. Before the war he had served various pastorates in his native South Carolina and had been professor of church history in the theological seminary at Columbia and an associate editor of the *Southern Presbyterian Review*. At the close of the war he went back to the First Presbyterian Church at New Orleans. Already known as a great pulpit orator, he seemed to his listeners to be more chastened and subdued than before. His hope seemed "humbler" as "with gentler persuasion he called for a revival of the Covenant of Grace."

But in the issues that grew out of the war, Benjamin Palmer remained for thirty-seven years a "superb Confederate." He began by opposing all efforts to unite Southern and Northern Presbyterians. In 1870 the Southern Assembly had before it a proposition from the Northern Assembly for unity, but Palmer would have none of it. The overture, he said, was "based on the fatal assumption that mutual grievances existed." But the North had no grievances to remedy: "Our records may be searched in vain for a single act of aggression, or a single unfriendly declaration against the Northern Church." The South, on the other hand, had much ground for complaint. In 1861 the Northern majority had changed the Presbyterian Church into a political organization, while the Southern Assembly was "non-political." In 1869, the peaceable reincorporation of the "New School" Presbyterians had made the Northern church into a "broad church, giving shelter to every creed." The Southern church would hold to the true faith. In addition, Palmer listed the Northern church's aberrance on matters of polity, cited jurisdictional disputes, and excoriated the Yankee apostates for ordaining Negroes. So long as Palmer lived there would be no Presbyterian unification.

Nor would Palmer yield greatly on other items in the Southern creed. In 1872 he appeared at the newly

renamed Washington and Lee University—where
the spirit of Lee gave reverential blessing to reconciliation and the New South—to speak on "The
Present Crisis and Its Issues." He took under con-
sideration what of the South's past should be retained and what surrendered. First of all, there was
the problem of race, and he was sure that it was "in-
dispensable that the purity of race should be preserved on either side." But he would accept, "as the
terms of National pacification," the Negro's emancipation and his political status—"however hastily or
unwisely conferred." Yet the "true policy" was that
the races should "stand apart in their own social
grade"—in their schools and in their churches—
while retaining the "kindness and helpful cooperation
of the old relations."

Then there was the labor question. Here Palmer
would compromise. "We must form a doctrine that
as an advanced civilization creates new wants and mul-
tiplies forms of industry, so *no species of labor* is *dis-
reputable* whose products swell the volume of that
civilization." But, even so, Palmer opposed all
"coarse and selfish utilitarianism" which measured
things by material standards. Facing monopolies,
Palmer deplored the subversion of the free market
to the "caprice of capitalists." And he abhorred the
degradation of public office from "a ministry of responsibility" to a "place of emolument." In it all he
saw a danger that the individual would be sacrificed

to concentrated power. "This," he proclaimed, "is one of the chief perils of the Republic."

With such a social philosophy, Palmer built his church until he had the largest congregation in New Orleans. He published his sermons each week and sold them in tremendous volume at ten cents a copy. He wrote works of biography and tracts on moral conduct. In the 1890's he launched a crusade against the Louisiana Lottery—"essentially an immoral institution" whose criminal business endangered the very existence of the state. His powerful voice had a large share in ending the institution. In addition, he sponsored a new Presbyterian university in the Southwest but refused its chancellorship. He opposed parochial schools, except when reconstruction measures had made them necessary for whites. Until his death, as the result of a streetcar accident in 1902, he remained staunchly loyal alike to the creed of the Old-School Presbyterians and the code of the Old South.

At the opposite corner of the Confederacy, another Presbyterian maintained the fundamentals of religious and Southern doctrine. Moses Drury Hoge was pastor of Richmond's Second Presbyterian Church, a close friend of Jefferson Davis, and an ardent admirer of that other strict Calvinist, Stonewall Jackson. During the war he had served as a volunteer chaplain in the Richmond camps; but his most spectacular service to his church and the Confederacy came in 1862, when he ran the blockade, made his way to England, and there collected 10,000 Bibles and 50,000 copies of the New Testament for the Confederate army. After the war, until his death in 1899, he served repeatedly as delegate to the conferences of the Evangelical Alliance in New York, Edinburgh, and Copenhagen. He was co-editor of the *Central Presbyterian* and ardent in promoting his denomination's cause. In 1875, at the invitation of the Virginia legislature, he made his most celebrated oratorical effort in dedicating a monument to his hero, Stonewall Jackson.

But Hoge's highest words of praise were for the Southern people, who, after exhibiting "valor and endurance" in war, had shown "patience and self-control," "dignity," and "heroic resignation" after the war. They would not again, Hoge promised, assert state sovereignty "by the sword"; but they had proved that the Yankees could not "conquer true greatness of soul." The preacher had full hopes that the future would vindicate the Southern cause.

Even more vigorous than the Presbyterians were a group of Confederate leaders in the Methodist ministry. Most forceful and ardent for the Lost Cause among them was Albert Taylor Bledsoe, who had served as assistant secretary of war in the Confederacy and as propagandist for the Confederate cause in England. Distantly related to Jefferson Davis' first wife, Bledsoe had had a long career in several professions before the Civil War. He had graduated from

West Point in 1830 but had resigned from the army two years later. He had studied law, theology, and philosophy for a time at Kenyon College and had taken orders in the Episcopal Church. For several years he had taught mathematics at Kenyon and at Miami University in Ohio. Then, for ten years, he had practiced law in Springfield, Illinois, learning to know well both Abraham Lincoln and Stephen A. Douglas. Finally he had returned to mathematics and had taught at the University of Mississippi. Secession had found him serving as professor of mathematics and astronomy at the University of Virginia.

After Appomattox, Bledsoe returned to the South from London, but he came back neither to his profession nor to his church. Instead, after a couple of years, he sought ordination in the Methodist Episcopal Church, South; and he founded and edited, from Baltimore, the *Southern Review,* "dedicated to the despised, disfranchised, and downtrodden people of the South." His first work, however, was a vindication of the South, slavery, and secession answering the query *Is Jefferson Davis a Traitor?*

The book, appearing in 1866 at a moment when Davis' case was uppermost in the public mind, was almost a sequel to Bledsoe's *Essay on Liberty and Slavery,* written a decade earlier. The earlier book, showing the influence of George Fitzhugh's *Sociology for the South,* elaborated upon the scriptural argument for slavery and insisted that slavery was a positive good. The essay on Jefferson Davis was a vigorous assertion of the legal right of secession and a vindication of Davis, Lee, Stonewall Jackson, and Albert Sidney Johnston from the ignorant aspersions of fanatical Yankees. These men were, all of them, "perfectly loyal to truth, justice, and the Constitution of 1787 as it came from the hands of the fathers."

The argument received further exposition in the pages of the *Southern Review*. In the magazine's first year Bledsoe published articles on "The Imprisonment of Davis," "The Legal Status of the Southern States," "The Origin of the Late War," "Southern War Poetry," "Chancellorsville," "The New America," "The North and the South," and "The North and the South in 1787." In addition, the editor took fourteen pages to denounce the errors in a Latin textbook, reviewed books on the history of philosophy, and excoriated Edward Everett. For Everett's doctrine that social disorders, being external, could be cured by external means, Bledsoe had only righteous scorn. It was a "doctrine of infidelity" that men could be "regenerated by new forms of society." On that doctrine could "grow no other than the bitter fruits of another French Revolution, another reign of terror, another pandemonium on earth."

Small wonder it was that a fellow Southerner found the *Review*, like its editor, "fearless, able, bold, gloveless, scholarly, distinctly Southern in thought and belligerently sectional." Small wonder, too, that the *Review* failed to attract subscribers. In 1871 Bledsoe begged the Methodists to take financial responsibility for the magazine and deplored the Southerners' indifference to their own literature. The Methodists, however, gave little aid, although Bledsoe continued until his death in 1877 to strike valiant blows against the heresies of Baptists and Presbyterians, against the political orientation of Northern Methodists, and against rationalistic philosophy, radical "brute force," industrialism, evolution, and all science which was an enemy of faith.

Other Methodist ministers among the Confederacy's leaders gave little attention, in the postwar period, to church affairs. Alfred Holt Colquitt, governor of Georgia and long a United States senator, was a licensed preacher of the Methodist Church. But after Appomattox his ecclesiastical activities were limited to a continuing interest in the Sunday School movement, while his major attention centered on Georgia politics and on industrial development. Rufus Garland, too, the brother of A. H. Garland and a Confederate congressman from Arkansas, was a Methodist minister; but his postwar career was important in neither church nor state. In 1882 he emerged as the Greenback candidate for governor of Arkansas, but his thousand-acre plantation absorbed most of his interest.

More significant both as a Methodist and as a nostalgic Confederate was Clement Anselm Evans, brigadier general from Georgia, who resolved in the midst of the war that it "was better to save men than to destroy them." At eighteen he had been a lawyer, at twenty-two a judge, at twenty-five a state senator. In 1865, when he was thirty-two years old, he applied to the Northern Georgia Conference for a license to preach. For the next twenty-five years he rode circuit in Georgia, trying to "teach men how to live together instead of murdering one another." In addition, he organized and was president of the Augusta and Summerville Land Company. In theology and in economics, he was noted for his willingness to accept the "true results of the war."

Yet, despite his capacity for adjustment, Evans was devoted to the Confederate memory. He commanded the Georgia Division of the United Confederate Veterans, and served as director and president of the Confederate Memorial Institute. He wrote *A Military History of Georgia* and edited the multivolumed *Confederate Military History*. Until his death in 1911 he was one of the most persistent historians of the Confederate glory. The Confederacy, he contended, had "the best form of constitutional government the world ever saw. Its administration had been able, humane, and considerate of the common welfare. Its leaders were among the most intellectual, cultured and patriotic of mankind." With reverence Evans endorsed the belief:

No nation ever rose so white and fair
None fell so pure of crime.

Another historian-ecclesiast, earnestly defending the Confederacy's purity, came from the Baptist ranks. John William Jones was a "fighting parson" in the ranks for one year of the war and then a chaplain of a Virginia regiment. In the series of revivals which swept Lee's armies—and which he later described in *Christ in the Camp*—he had a leading part. Immediately after the war, he arrived in Lexington, Virginia, as pastor of the Baptist Church. General Lee's deep interest in the spiritual development of Washington College's students led him to invite the local ministers to occupy, in turn, the pulpit of the college chapel. Thus, Jones could claim that he was "chaplain" of the college, while his contact with Lee furnished him with materials for his *Personal Reminiscences of General R. E. Lee* and his *Life and Letters of Robert E. Lee*. His acquaintance with Lee did not, however, convert him to a New South philosophy. Nor did a succession of other pastorates or even a post as agent for the Southern Baptist Theological Seminary at Louisville distract him from giving whole-souled devotion to the Confederacy. He wrote "The Morale of the Confederate Army" for Evans' *Military History*, edited a memorial volume for the Army of Northern Virginia and another for Jefferson Davis, and wrote *A School History of the*

United States, giving the truth of history from the Southern standpoint. From 1876 to 1887 he was secretary of the Southern Historical Society and editor of its polemic publications. From 1890 to his death in 1909 he was chaplain general of the United Confederate Veterans.

Considerably less devoted to Confederate reminiscence and to the philosophy of the Old South were a group of Episcopal priests among the Confederate leaders. The Protestant Episcopal Church had not been as torn by the sectional controversy as had the more popular sects, and Episcopalians found the road back to national ecclesiastic unity reasonably smooth. The autonomous nature of the state-bounded dioceses eliminated the jurisdictional disputes which hampered unity in other denominations, while theological controversies within the church had not taken on a sectional coloration. At the first convention of the church after the war, the Northerners—who had sanely refrained from reading the Southern bishops out of the church—invited the Southerners to attend. The Southerners returned to the fold with only a minimum of friction and an almost complete absence of recrimination. Leading the movement was Henry Champlin Lay, missionary bishop to the Southwest, who had served, without commission, as chaplain in the Confederate armies. The first postwar convention of the Episcopalians made him bishop of Arkansas; and four years later, upon the division of the New

York diocese, he became bishop of Easton, with headquarters in Baltimore. A gifted theologian and devoted churchman, he wasted little time bemoaning the Lost Cause.

Two Confederate brigadier generals, William Nelson Pendleton and Ellison Capers, devoted their postwar years to the Episcopal Church. Pendleton, scion of a distinguished Virginia family, returned to Grace Church in Lexington, Virginia—the parish he had left to become the chief of artillery in the Army of Northern Virginia. Before the war he had risen to greater prominence in his church than the smallness of his parish would indicate. He had graduated from West Point in 1830 and returned after a year in the artillery to teach mathematics in the Academy. In 1833 he resigned to become professor of mathematics at Bristol College, which evangelical Episcopalians were organizing. The school failed in four years, but in the meantime Pendleton had taken holy orders. He became, momentarily, a professor at Newark College in Delaware; and then in 1839, at the instance of Bishop William Meade, he founded the Episcopal High School of Virginia at Alexandria. After five years he resigned from the debt-ridden school to return to parish work. By 1853 he was at Grace Church, devoting his spare time to ferreting out heresies and preparing a volume which found *Science a Witness for the Bible*.

Returned to Lexington, Pendleton soon had

Robert E. Lee as his most distinguished communicant and senior warden of his vestry. The two men closely resembled each other, and the priest was often mistaken for the college president. Both men came from the Virginia aristocracy. Both were reserved in manner. Beneath Pendleton's "somewhat haughty stamp" his intimates detected a "temper naturally simple, kindly and generous." He was an abler scholar than his senior warden, but a poorer administrator. His knowledge of mathematics, the classics, and theology exceeded his knowledge of men. Man of positive opinions and eager and formidable debater though he was, his friends nevertheless knew that he was "as guileless as a child" and an uncritical donor to every old soldier with a hard-luck tale.

On the issues of reconciliation, Pendleton followed Lee with considerable reluctance. His Confederate commission excluded him from amnesty, and in June, 1865, when he returned to his parish, he refused to read the established prayer for the president of the United States. The military authorities promptly closed his church, and for several months the parishioners met secretly in private homes. To a federal commissioner, Pendleton declared that "honesty compels me to add that my own convictions remain wholly unchanged respecting the rights of the States" and the wrongs inflicted upon the South. "As it has, however, pleased the Almighty Ruler of the world to permit us to be overwhelmed, I accept the necessity of the position and am willing to submit myself peaceably to an authority which, however I think of its justice, I cannot resist to any good purpose."

Before Lee arrived at Grace Church, Pendleton had taken the oath and applied for pardon. He aided in returning the diocese of Virginia to the church— though he admitted that "the necessity of the step grieves me." Thereafter he threw himself into the work of the church and, burying his pride, went North to seek funds for enlarging his building. Hardly had he performed the last sad rites over the body of General Lee when he hurried into the deep South to solicit money for a Lee Memorial Church.

Yet with all his personal devotion to his old commander, General Pendleton never followed Robert E. Lee into full acceptance of the new social order. He filed no protest in the name of the revered Marse Robert when Jefferson Davis wrote him complainingly: "My efforts to vindicate their cause will find, therefore, little favor with this generation. Perhaps they may arraign me for disturbing the harmony about which they prate, and of which the only evidence is to be found in their humiliating concessions." He agreed, in fact, with Davis, but he ignored the controversy whenever possible. He built his church with a fierce intensity, finding in the Kingdom of Heaven a means of escaping the memories of the Lost Cause.

Like Pendleton in Virginia, Ellison Capers in South

Carolina turned his energies to the church after the war. Like Pendleton, too, Capers had been educated in a military school—The Citadel—and had been a professor of mathematics. His father was a Methodist bishop, famed in the annals of his church for his missionary work among the slaves. Professor Capers, however, showed no interest in the ministry until the experiences of the Civil War, in which he rose from major to brigadier general, turned his thoughts to religion. Legend had it that as the tide of battle at Chickamauga threatened to annihilate his command, he vowed to devote his life to the church if God would extricate his men from the portending massacre. Returning to civil life, he was elected secretary of state under the provisional government, but a political career in harassed South Carolina had no appeal to him. Nor did the turbulent controversies, political, social, and theological, of his father's denomination. The younger Capers, still under thirty, turned to the Episcopal Church, studied for the priesthood, and surrendered the great seal of South Carolina to Francis Cardoza, his able Negro successor.

He became rector of Christ Church in Greenville, and for twenty years—except for a brief interlude in Selma, Alabama—he ministered to a parish which included Negro as well as white communicants. Although he had left his father's church, Capers did not abandon his father's work. He took pride in the missionary work he was able to carry on among the freedmen, directing the work of gathering Negroes into the fold, and supervising the missionary activities of the diocese. In 1887 he became rector of Trinity Church, Columbia, and six years later he was consecrated bishop of South Carolina. In 1904 he became chancellor of the University of the South. Two years later, as age and multiplied duties forced him to accept a coadjutor bishop, he explained to his diocesan council that he would assign other duties to his assistant, but he would retain control over the missions and schools for the colored people. "I feel a deep interest in the moral, material, and spiritual welfare of our colored brethren," he later explained as he advocated setting the Negro churches under their own bishops.

But churchly interests and ministering to the Negroes did not consume all of Bishop Capers' attention. He found time, too, for reminiscence. He was active among the United Confederate Veterans and wrote South Carolina's story for Evans' *Confederate Military History*. It was reminiscence without bitterness, and veterans' affairs were only an avocation. Perhaps Capers followed the example of Robert E. Lee more completely than any ecclesiastic among the Confederate leaders.

If there was exception, it was Capers' opposite number in the Roman Catholic Church. Patrick K. Lynch, bishop of Charleston and editor of the *Catholic Miscellany,* was a dogmatic writer of polemic force and a preacher whose Irish tongue easily scaled the heights of traditional Southern oratory. In 1861 fire destroyed his residence, his cathedral, and other church property. Yet in 1863 the bishop took time to carry a personal letter from President Davis to the Holy Father and to press for the Vatican's good will to the Confederate States. Still in Rome when the war ended, the bishop received Secretary of State W. H. Seward's permission to return. Back in Charleston he found that William T. Sherman's armies had brought more destruction to convents and churches, while the diocesan debt had grown to $220,000. Promptly the bishop began to rebuild and hurried into the North to preach the dogma of reconciliation and collect funds to resuscitate the church in South Carolina. Ecclesiastical finance made necessary a new political philosophy; and so successfully did Patrick, bishop of Charleston, capitalize upon his self-conferred title, "Ambassador of Good Will," that he liquidated before 1882 all but $15,000 of his war-born debt.

Neither philosophy nor financial need brought another Catholic priest to reconciliation. Father Abram Joseph Ryan was a sentimentalist rather than a dogmatist, and he volunteered as a chaplain in the Confederate service without deep convictions on the political or social issues. His war poems "In Memory of My Brother" and "In Memoriam" touched a popular chord of romantic sentiment in the Southern heart.

For a dozen years after the war his lyric sadness expressed the depression of Southern folk:

> Furl that Banner, softly, slowly!
> Treat it gently—it is holy—
> For it droops above the dead.
> Touch it not—unfold it never—
> Let it droop there, furled forever,
> For its people's hopes are dead.

But sentiment, as well as economics or philosophy, could work a change. In 1887 Northern aid to cholera sufferers touched the heart of the poet-priest, and he forgave:

> Blessings on thine every wave,
>   Blessings on thine every shore,
> Blessings that from sorrow save,
>   Blessings giving more and more,
> For all thou gavest thy sister land,
> O Northland in thy generous deed and grand.

Not all, by any means, of the ordained churchmen among the leading Confederates occupied pulpits. Many of them were educators serving as administrators or teachers in the denominational colleges which dotted the South. Like their colleagues in the parishes, they faced the issues of reconstruction; evaluated the new problems of the Negro, industrialization, and a changing social order; and made their choices between preserving the heritage of the Old South and embracing the promises of the New South. Strategically placed to influence the thinking of a newer generation, they exhibited no greater unanimity than did their brethren in the pulpits. Some of them taught the new precepts of reconciliation, while others cast an aura of sanctity and scholarship over an attitude of intransigence.

Symbolic, perhaps, of the clashing ideologies of the postwar years was the career of the University of the South. On the eve of the Civil War the Protestant Episcopal dioceses of ten Southern states, under the aggressive leadership of Louisiana's Bishop Leonidas Polk, united to found a Southern university which would be "the noblest and best endowed in Christendom." On October 10, 1860, a scant month before Lincoln's election, in the center of a "Domain" of ten thousand acres atop Sewanee Mountain, before eight bishops, two hundred priests, and five thousand spectators, Bishop Polk laid the cornerstone of the first building of the University of the South. Already, in its constitution, Polk and the trustees had laid the foundation plans for a curriculum broader than that of any American university then existing. There were to be "schools" of Greek, Latin, and mathematics; of physics, and of metaphysics; of history, and of natural science; of geology, civil engineering, experimental chemistry, agriculture, and agricultural chemistry; of moral science; of English and French and German and Spanish and Italian, and of oriental language and literature; of the philosophy of languages, and of the philosophy of education; of rhetoric, American his-

tory, geography, astronomy, political science, commerce, theology, law, medicine, mining, and fine arts!

It was a program of magnificent potentialities, but
fate prevented its realization. Lincoln was elected,
and hostile armies encamped on Sewanee Mountain
destroyed the cornerstone. And on a June morning in
1864, on top of another mountain in neighboring
Georgia, a cannon ball stopped the great heart of
Lieutenant General Leonidas Polk, C.S.A. The
plan the bishop-general had fathered fell under the eye
of Colonel William Preston Johnston, Episcopalian
and professor of English at Washington College. In
modified form it became the basis for President Lee's
recommendations to his trustees!

On Tennessee's Sewanee Mountain were only the
refuse left by careless soldiers and the ash heap
marking the hopeful homes which Bishops Polk,
Stephen Elliott, and James H. Otey had built. Bishop
Otey, too, official "chancellor" of the unborn University of the South, was dead. Only the dream of the
University lived on—lived on in the mind of Charles
Todd Quintard, who, in September, 1865, was elected
bishop of Tennessee.

Connecticut-born Charles Quintard had been educated in medicine, and was professor of physiology in
the Medical College of Memphis when he sought ordination, in 1856, in the Episcopal Church. A Unionist, who in November of 1860 preached on "Obedience to Rulers," he left his Nashville church to serve

as chaplain in the Confederate armies. Five months after his return, a convention of the diocese named him bishop; and a month later, at the general convention of the reunited church, Southern and Northern bishops joined in consecrating him to the episcopacy. "I felt," said the new bishop, "that the war between the States was indeed over."

Assuming his duties in Tennessee, Quintard lost no time in reviving the University of the South. Lest the land revert to the donors, he hurried to Sewanee Mountain. In March of 1866 he erected a cross and selected sites for buildings and a chapel. In October he assembled the trustees and accepted the position of vice-chancellor of the university. He selected a business manager and opened a preparatory department. Then he began to search for money.

In Charleston, Bishop Lynch of the Roman Church, seeking to rebuild his devastated diocese, sought his funds in the North, becoming an ambassador of good will and an apostle of reconciliation. Every superficial aspect in Bishop Quintard's career—his Connecticut birth, his Northern education, his Unionism, his consecration as a symbol of a reunited church—pointed out a similar course for the bishop of Tennessee. Even his medical training might conceivably have predisposed him toward the scientific, "practical" aspects of Bishop Polk's plan. But beneath these superficialities, Dr. Quintard was a High-Church mystic. In addition to the university, he interested himself in establishing sisterhoods, in the cathedral movement, in perpetuating the Gothic style in church architecture, and in the Oxford movement with its emphasis on ritualism. He was one of the first clergymen to wear an academic hood with his vestments. "The idea," indignantly exclaimed a Low-Church lady in Connecticut on one occasion, "of that Southern Bishop coming to this church and wearing a Rebel flag on his back."

It was not, however, a rebel flag. It was a British one. Instead of turning northward with submissive words of reconciliation, Dr. Quintard went to London. He attended the Lambeth Conference, preached in St. Paul's, laid cornerstones, won encomiums from the British press, and came home with $8,700 for his university. Four more times before his death in 1889 Bishop Quintard went to England soliciting aid. One obstacle, he sadly told his closest friend in Tennessee, "I meet with everywhere, 'why doesn't your rich North help you?'" Repeatedly the British suggested that Northern dioceses should aid. "Of course," complained the bishop, "there is an answer but I have to make it constantly."

Whatever the answer, Bishop Quintard built his university on English models with only a minimum of Yankee gold. He built Gothic buildings on Sewanee Mountain; he took pride that men could say, "Probably nowhere else in America is there any such formal and stately Collegiate ceremony as at Sewanee"; and he strove to "teach all those things which a Christian ought to know and believe to his soul's health." He established a theological school and turned the preparatory department into a military academy. But, except for short-lived schools of commerce, medicine, and law, the broad-ranging dream of Bishop Polk found no resting place on the "Domain." Bishop Quintard had actually established, on a British rather than a Yankee model, a university of the Old South. Bishop Polk's plan did, however, inspire Colonel William Preston Johnston, who, after inducing General Lee to accept it, carried it with him when he became president of Louisiana State and later of Tulane.

In Dr. Quintard's university some of the leaders of the Confederacy—Josiah Gorgas and Edmund Kirby-Smith among them—found refuge. Among them, too, was Florida's young Brigadier General Francis Asbury Shoup, a West Point graduate who had practiced law in Indianapolis before the war. In 1865 he was made professor of mathematics at the University of Mississippi. Soon he took orders and became rector, as well, of St. Peter's Episcopal Church in Oxford. But the government of Mississippi changed, and a Republican board member censured Professor Shoup for permitting a student orator to criticize the Radical Congress of the United States. Under fire, General Shoup resigned and went on the mountain, where Dr. Quintard made him professor of mathematics and chaplain of the university.

After five years Shoup ventured down and served parishes in New York, Nashville, and New Orleans. But from 1883 to 1896 he was back at Sewanee as professor of mathematics. His intellectual capacity was great, but his metaphysical speculations were usually beyond his students' grasp.

Another who came to Sewanee was Brigadier General Josiah Gorgas, chief of ordnance who wrought the miracle of keeping the Confederate armies supplied with arms and ammunition. A West Point graduate and an accomplished engineer, he became superintendent of the ironworks at Brierfield, Alabama, when the Confederacy collapsed. But four years later he joined Dr. Quintard, becoming headmaster of the preparatory school. When the college department began, he became professor of engineering, and in 1872 he assumed the duties of vicechancellor. Six years later he accepted the presidency of the University of Alabama, but he held the post only one year. "Ill health," at least officially, forced his retirement to the position of librarian, which he held until his death in 1883.

Although the founding of the University of the South was perhaps the most significant event in the postwar history of religious education, Dr. Quintard was by no means the only ecclesiastic among the Confederate leaders to turn to education. Among the Baptists, three Confederate leaders gave attention to schools. South Carolina's Congressman Lewis M.

Ayer, Harvard graduate, lawyer, planter, and state legislator, had had such enthusiasm for the Southern cause that he equipped and led a company to Kansas in the fifties. Ardent secessionist and member of the secession convention, he served both terms in the Confederate Congress as a valiant supporter of President Davis. After the war he became a cotton factor in Charleston, and then returned to his plantation, where his 200 Negroes had faithfully remained. Soon, unknown to his family, he began to study the Bible; and before the end of 1869 he joined the Baptist Church. In 1872 he entered the ministry as pastor of the Baptist Church in Anderson. Three years later he accepted a call to Texas; but he soon returned, stopping to study for a session at the theological seminary at Greenville, and then accepting a pastorate at Murfreesboro, Tennessee. In 1879 he returned to Anderson to establish a female seminary. A man of magnificent appearance, great-bearded like one of the ancient prophets, Ayer won the love of the young through his kindness and gained the respect of the mature through his wisdom and encyclopedic knowledge. Even when age brought retirement from his pastoral and administrative duties, he continued to teach as professor of mental and moral science, geology, and political economy in the Patrick Military Institute.

Another Baptist minister who founded a woman's college was Brigadier General Mark P. Lowrey, famed for a motto of conduct, "Preach like Hell on

Sunday and fight like the Devil all week." He returned to the ministry at the close of the war, worked
diligently to revive churches which had suffered from
the war, and served for a decade as president of the
Mississippi Baptist Convention. In 1873 he founded
the Blue Mountain Female Institute, which he ran as
a private school closely connected with the denomination. He was president and professor of history and
moral science. His work aided the advancement of
education for women in Mississippi. He served, too,
for a four-year term on the board of trustees for the
state university.

While Ayer and Lowrey were stimulating education
for women, James Petigru Boyce, sometime professor of systematic theology, Confederate army chaplain, state legislator, and member of the staff of South
Carolina's governor, was reviving and improving theological education. Early Baptist ministerial education had been haphazard, and men like General Lowrey had had no formal schooling. Boyce, a graduate
of Brown University, had raised the theological department of Furman College to independent status
as the Southern Baptist Theological Seminary. After
the war Boyce returned to the school, paid its debts
by the sale of his inherited plantations, and revived
its work. Moving the seminary to Louisville, he built
it into the leading school of the Southern denomination and a staunch bulwark of conservative Baptist
and Southern principles.

Even more vigorous defenders of theological and Southern orthodox dogmas were two Presbyterian educators, Richard McIlwaine and Robert Louis Dabney—both chaplains with Stonewall Jackson and both high in the military and social hierarchy of the Confederacy. McIlwaine had been educated at Hampden-Sydney College, graduated in law at the University of Virginia, and trained in theology in Union Theological Seminary and the Free Church College of Edinburgh. For eighteen years after the war he served churches in Farmville and Lynchburg and worked as secretary of the Southern Presbyterian Church's board of missions. In 1883, at the age of fifty, he assumed the presidency and the chair of moral philosophy and Bible studies at the almost defunct Hampden-Sydney. Until his retirement in 1904, he worked to build the institution, increase its endowment, and maintain its standards. He succeeded in bringing its student body back to its prewar numbers —116 students. Few in number though the students were, President McIlwaine labored diligently to hold them to right-minded doctrine. Once, when he found a class uncritically accepting the "unhistorical, irrational, unscriptural" teachings on slavery as presented in a textbook on "Christian Ethics," he summoned the members to an extra, evening session in his study. For three hours he labored with them, until they "had come to an understanding and adoption of the Southern point of view." President McIlwaine was convinced that "one of the foremost obligations resting on our Southern instructors in morals is to see that their students are grounded on those eternal principles of truth and right for which their fathers stood." In 1901, still firm in that belief, he served in Virginia's constitutional convention on the committee on education, and created the state's central board of education. In and out of the convention he insisted on educational tests for suffrage.

It was President McIlwaine's old teacher of theology, Robert Louis Dabney, who more vigorously than any other Southern teacher conformed to McIlwaine's definition of an instructor's duty. A chaplain serving as chief of staff under Stonewall Jackson, Dabney shared his chief's undeviating devotion to the Southern cause. Saddened by Jackson's death and by the Confederacy's collapse, Dabney returned to his professorship of theology at Union Theological Seminary a bitter man. Serving without pay, farming to raise his own food, he saw no gleam of hope for the South. Indignantly he repudiated an offer to teach at Yankee Princeton; and for a lustrum he dreamed of emigration to Brazil, Australia, or anywhere that Southern Christianity could strike new roots. Failing to find a haven beyond the South, Dabney devoted thirty years to saving the South from succumbing to infidel and unconstitutional Northern ideas.

In his church, Dr. Dabney was a staunch opponent

of Presbyterian unity. Both because the Northern churches were unsound on matters of doctrine and because they contained "a holy mob of abolitionists" who "would have dragged them right out of the church, and for the greater glory of God, murdered their 'dear Southern brethren' in the streets," Dabney denounced unification. In 1870 he harangued the General Assembly in Louisville for three hours—until the unifiers fled in terror. "He stripped every leaf from the olive branch and made it a rod to beat us with," ruefully reported one of the chastized. Steadily, through the years, Dabney stood guard against Yankee infiltration. He opposed joining a Pan-Presbyterian alliance, opposed "fraternal correspondence," opposed sending fraternal delegates to Northern meetings.

Yet even in his own seminary, Dr. Dabney fought a losing fight. Not even his colleagues at Union Seminary could be brought up to his strict principles. They succumbed to the virus of unity, and in 1882 the movement for Presbyterian reconciliation made headway. Sick and disgusted, Dr. Dabney prepared to leave the seminary. "I knew," he declared, "that when it became a Yankee institution, under Yankee church government, the rebel and traitor Dabney would not be retained as professor." He foresaw, too, that Northern seminaries would draw off students, and Union would "sink into a contemptible decline." Defiantly, he departed for the University of Texas to spend another decade as professor of mental and moral philosophy and political economy. Within a year after his arrival in Austin he had founded the Austin Theological Seminary as a new fortress of Presbyterian truth.

"Rebel and traitor" by his own definition, Dabney's rebellion against the forces of Yankee reconstruction and the pressures of the New South extended beyond Presbyterian doctrine and polity. He had been a Unionist before the war and had joined the Confederacy only because of the righteousness of the Southern cause and the wickedness of the North. Before the war was over, he was at work on a biography of his beloved Jackson, and part of the book was published in England before Appomattox. The volume appeared in 1866, with a defiant preface asserting that Southerners believed state sovereignty "absolutely essential as the bulwark of the liberties of the people." Force convinced them they could not save that doctrine. But the oath he had taken to obey the government of the United States "did not bind me to think or to say the principles on which I had acted were erroneous; but to abstain, in future, from the assertion of them by force of arms."

The next year, Dr. Dabney published *A Defense of Virginia*, reviewing once again the question of slavery. This was, in fact, the last major formal statement of the proslavery argument. It recounted the familiar arguments—historical, biological, economic, consti-

tutional, and scriptural—for slavery. Dabney justified the Virginia penal code's discrimination against
Negroes on the grounds that black men had a "lower
moral tone." He declared the Emancipation Proclamation "the most violent economic measure ever attempted in history," and he showed—from figures of
a declining Negro population—that emancipation
hurt Negroes worse than whites. It was, of course, to
be expected that the North would next seek to impose
Negro suffrage, Negro officeholding, and Negro su-
periority. The tyrant section would use more and
more violent inducements to bribe the Negroes, with
additional gifts, to aid in Yankee domination. Amalgamation, he prophesied, would result; and in the
distant future he foresaw a hybrid race, incapable of
carrying on civilization, dragging down the North
through "disorganizing heresies" and inevitable
anarchy. This would, eventually and at a horrible
cost, avenge the South.

Already Dabney was making a valiant fight against
Negro amalgamation in the Presbyterian Church. Before the synod of Virginia in 1867 he unloosed a
passionate philippic against admitting Negroes to the
church ordination, and ultimately the Presbyterians
set up a separate African organization. From New
Orleans, the Reverend Dr. Palmer sent his whole-
souled approbation. To Dr. Hoge, Dabney moaned
that he saw all his apprehensions verified—"and espe-

cially the worst of them, the emasculation of the spirit and honor of our people."

Not only did Dabney oppose Negro ordination; he opposed Negro education as well. In 1876 he alleged that a Negro did not need a common-school education to fit him to exercise the suffrage, since he would soon lose the right to vote. Education would, therefore, only encourage the Negroes in idleness, inefficiency, and immorality. Three years later he expanded his opposition to Negro education to include all public education. The state, he asserted, was incompetent to give an education of a desirable moral character, and it was only a delusion to think of educating all men. After all, education of the youth was a responsibility of the parents. He would, however, assent to educating "aspiring" Negroes from a separate literary fund. The fund, like that of the whites, should be raised by separate taxation—"let each tub stand upon its own bottom."

At the University of Texas, Dr. Dabney continued to expand and to expound these ideas. He wrote articles on educational problems, commentaries on politics, and volumes on theology. He was an earnest teacher, holding students to the highest standards. Despite the rigidity of his principles, he kept an active mind. He tested the developments of the times by the standards of the highest morality. He was skeptical of science and opposed to the doctrine of evolution. He opposed labor unions and strikes—insisting that the state should suppress the criminal conspiracies of workers with "as firm and prompt a hand" as it would put down highway robbery. He found the agricultural depression of the early 1890's a natural result of the overthrow of the old labor system of the South, the protective tariff, and class legislation favoring monopolies. He opposed both the money oligarchy and the free coinage of silver, worked out an independent theory of the currency, and proposed that Congress pass a bill treating both gold and silver as commodities.

Eventually the time came in Texas—as it had at Union Seminary—when Dr. Dabney's rigid standards, orthodox and conservative views, and forthright pronouncements brought opposition. In 1894 a reorganized board asked his resignation from the university. Age and blindness, said the official version, made it impossible for him to do his work. Protesting, the old professor gave up his post; and four years later, at the age of seventy-eight, he died. He belonged, said a commentator a few years later, to the "old order of faith and reason." He was "at war with atheistic and infidel theories of physical science which have so largely prevailed, with the various forms of evolution, anti-biblical in their essence. He knew that man was never evolved from ape." But, said the commentator—he was writing in the *Nation* in 1904— "the fact that men like him possessed unsullied in-

tegrity, severe conscientiousness, and an utter lack of
selfish ambition but added to the harm they were able
to do by keeping their countrymen out of the great
spiritual currents of the present century." Dr. Dabney might well have considered the comment a com-
pliment; he was, in truth, the last, the greatest, and
the most courageous defender of the "faith and
reason" of the Old South.

Not all the Confederate leaders who turned to education in the postwar years were clergymen. The
ministers were, in fact, only a minority. The majority
were military men who found new careers in educational administration or in teaching. The American
custom of elevating former army officers to administrative posts in higher education received its greatest impetus in the postwar South. General Lee was
only the first among the many who turned their military talents into academic service.

For the most part, too, the soldiers who turned
educators followed Lee's example of readjusting to
new conditions. The ecclesiastics, in general, clung
to the values of the Old South. They had lived by
"faith and reason," and their principles survived military defeat. They belonged in the valiant band that
stood with Jefferson Davis. But the military men
had lived by the sword; they had staked their cause
on the arbitrament of battle, and they were willing
to abide its result. They lived with memories of their

martial glory, but remembrance seldom led to recalcitrance. They followed the example of Lee, making —each according to his talents—a part of the New South.

In addition to General Lee, two lieutenant generals, six major generals, two brigadier generals, two naval officers, one senator, and three Confederate congressmen became presidents—at some time or other—of Southern colleges and universities. One major general and five brigadier generals became principals of high schools or military academies, while two brigadier generals were state superintendents of schools and one was superintendent of the city schools of Norfolk. In addition, seven brigadier generals became college professors, and three taught in secondary schools. Three naval officers, six congressmen (one of whom left the South to teach at De Veaux College in Niagara Falls), one senator, two judges, an assistant secretary of state, a commissioner to Russia, and an attorney general of Virginia held academic chairs. For the most part, the civilians taught law— though there were one historian and one obstetrician among them—and the military men taught mathematics and related subjects—though one brigadier general taught agriculture, one taught medicine, and one was a professor of English.

The institutions which these quondam Confederate leaders served covered the entire South. The University of Arkansas had Lieutenant General Daniel Harvey Hill—who abandoned teaching after the war to edit ill-fated magazines for a dozen years—for its president from 1877 to 1884. General Hill had graduated from West Point but had resigned from the army to teach mathematics, first at Washington College and then at Davidson College. After the war he published a magazine, *The Land We Love,* devoted to vindicating the South. In its pages the general called for changes in education. The mistake of the Old South had been its educational emphasis on politics and on the classics. Its new needs were for science, for the practical and the useful: "We must make a total radical change in our system of education." He accepted the presidency of the Arkansas Industrial University determined to elevate science and the mechanic arts to their proper place. From 1885 to 1889 General Hill was superintendent of the Middle Georgia Military and Agricultural College.

In Texas, Confederate Chief Justice Oran M. Roberts ran a law school until he was elected governor. During his administration, 1878–1882, the University of Texas was created; and upon conclusion of his term, he joined the faculty as professor of law. Another Texas governor, Brigadier General Lawrence S. Ross, moved from the governorship to the presidency of Texas Agricultural and Mechanical College. In the Louisiana State University, Rear Admiral Raphael Semmes served a brief year as professor of moral philosophy and English literature,

Confederate Senator Thomas Jenkins Semmes was professor of civil law for six years, and Brigadier General Allen Thomas was professor of agriculture for two years in the eighties until President Grover Cleveland made him coiner of the New Orleans mint.

In Mississippi, Lieutenant General A. P. Stewart was chancellor of the state university for the dozen terms between 1874 and 1886, and one-legged Brigadier General Claudius W. Sears was professor of mathematics. There, too, for a brief interlude in his political career, Lucius Q. C. Lamar, Confederate commissioner to Russia, taught law by the new case method.

General Stewart, "Old Straight" to his soldiers, had taught mathematics at Cumberland University before the war. He had opposed slavery and secession, and, when the war closed, was fully prepared for reconciliation. But the iniquities of "Parson" William Gannaway Brownlow's regime in Tennessee disgusted him. In 1870, he left Cumberland University to become secretary of the Mutual Life Insurance Company of St. Louis, lured by an annual salary of $8,000. He welcomed the chance of returning to education, however, and enjoyed his years in Oxford. During his administration women were admitted to "Ole Miss" for the first time. In 1890 he became one of the commissioners of the Chickamauga National Park. Always pious, in his old age he became a follower of Pastor Tazewell Russell and supported the Jehovah's Witnesses. As he surveyed the world from

Pastor Russell's watchtower, he was indeed convinced that the Biblical "great time of trouble" would soon be upon the earth. Pastor Russell predicted that the "Great Tribulation" would begin in 1914, but General Stewart did not live to see it. He died six years earlier at the age of eighty-seven.

In another part of the state, Major General Stephen Dill Lee presided, from 1880 to 1899, over the Mississippi Agricultural and Mechanical College. A West Point man without previous educational experience, he had spent a dozen years after the war as a planter. In 1878 he was in the state senate when the bill creating the A. and M. College passed. Selected as its first president, General Lee promptly defined the aim of the college to be "a thorough English education, with a practical knowledge of the sciences that underlie Agriculture and Mechanic Arts." The youth, he said, "are ripe for Industrial Education" and must be prepared for "the great industrial future just ahead in Mississippi and the Southern States." For nineteen years General Lee resisted all efforts to introduce the classics, philosophy, or any other distracting subjects. He carried on agricultural education, promoted experiments with cottonseed by-products, and encouraged diversified agriculture and drainage. Before he resigned to accept a place on the Vicksburg Park Commission, he had made enormous contributions to the development of practical education in Mississippi. He was, in addition, an ardent member of the Baptist Church, a promoter and first president of the state historical society, and an enthusiastic commander of the United Confederate Veterans. He died in 1908 at the age of seventy-five.

In Georgia, in addition to Lieutenant General D. H. Hill at the Georgia Military College, there was Brigadier General George Washington Rains as professor of chemistry and pharmacy and sometime dean at the Medical College of Georgia, Assistant Secretary of State William M. Browne as professor of history at the University of Georgia, and Confederate Congressman D. W. Lewis as president of the North Georgia Agricultural College. Congressman Clifford Anderson taught law in Mercer University. South Carolina had Congressman William Porcher Miles for two years, 1880–1882, as president of the university and Senator R. W. Barnwell as chairman of the faculty, professor of history, and eventually librarian at the university. For a brief time Brigadier General Edward Porter Alexander was professor of mathematics. From 1885 to 1890 Brigadier General George D. Johnston was superintendent of The Citadel.

But for three brigadier generals, R. E. Colston, who briefly ran a military academy in Wilmington; Evander M. Law, who founded the South Florida Military Institute; and T. F. Toon, who was for a time North Carolina's state superintendent of public instruction, Florida and North Carolina educational institutions gave no places to Confederate leaders. Brigadier General W. F. Perry taught English in Ogden College at Bowling Green, Kentucky. Two naval officers, Admiral Franklin Buchanan and Captain W. H. Parker, served terms as president of the Maryland Agricultural College.

Two institutions in Tennessee and three in Virginia welcomed the former leaders of the Confederacy. When Lieutenant General Edmund Kirby-Smith returned from Mexico and Cuba late in 1865, he sought a means of supporting his family. For two years, he was busy organizing and promoting the Atlantic and Pacific Telegraph Company in Louisville and serving as president of an accident insurance company. Neither venture proving profitable, he established a military school at New Castle, Kentucky. In 1870 fire destroyed his buildings. Then, in partnership with Major General Bushrod R. Johnson, he contracted with the trustees of the University of Nashville to revive that institution. General Kirby-Smith assumed the chancellorship and General Johnson became principal of the academic department. The two generals agreed to share the profits equally. But there were no profits, and after five hopeless years of competing with the newly created Vanderbilt, the trustees turned the property over to the Peabody Normal Institute. General Johnson spent his last five years on an Indiana farm, but General Kirby-Smith, who had become a lay reader and who thought of being ordained, ascended Bishop Quintard's mountain. There, secure in the "Domain" of the University of the South, the commander of the last Confederate army to surrender remained as professor of mathematics, supporting his eleven children on a salary of $1,400 to $1,800 a year, serving as lay reader, and gathering and classifying the flora of the Cumberlands. He had forgiven his country's enemies, and he had found a haven of refuge. He died on March 28, 1893, and his last words were a summary of his days: "Yea, though I walk through the valley of the shadow of death, I will fear no evil."

Virginia's three harbors for ex-Confederate leaders were the Virginia Polytechnic Institute, the Virginia Military Institute, and the renamed Washington and Lee University. The first was clearly a "New South" institution, founded in 1872 to take advantage of the Morrill Land Grant Acts and to furnish scientific and technical education. On its first faculty was Brigadier General James H. Lane, graduate of V.M.I. and the University of Virginia and onetime teacher of mathematics and tactics at V.M.I., who had charged with Pickett at Gettysburg and commanded the rear guard as Lee fell back into Virginia. After Appomattox he had walked to his North Carolina home, worked as a laborer until he could borrow $150, and then sought re-employment as a teacher. He welcomed the post of professor of natural philosophy and commandant at V.P.I. and served there until "politics" forced him out in 1881. In 1882 he became professor of civil engineering at Alabama Polytechnic Institute in Auburn, serving until his death in 1908. In 1875 Brigadier General William R. Boggs left a varied career as civil engineer on railroads to become professor of mechanics at V.P.I. He, too, left in 1881. Four years later, while Major General Fitzhugh Lee was governor of Virginia, Major General L. L. Lomax, who had been farming for twenty years, became president of V.P.I. He served until 1899 and then joined the War Department staff, compiling the *Official Records of the War of the Rebellion.*

The Virginia Military Institute, which had furnished many army leaders to the Confederacy, provided surprisingly few postwar berths for top-ranking Confederates. Major General George Washington Custis Lee followed his father to Lexington and held the professorship of civil and military engineering at V.M.I. until 1871. The only other Confederate leaders at V.M.I. were two naval officers: Commander Matthew Fontaine Maury and John Mercer Brooks. Maury, who had gained prewar fame as a geographer, served the Confederacy in Europe. He remained abroad, in Mexico and England, until 1868, when he accepted a position as professor of meteorology at V.M.I. He lectured occasionally but taught no classes. Instead, he devoted the last four years of his life to a physical survey of Virginia. Distinctly a devotee of the New South, he criticized

Southern education because of its devotion to the classics. As against Latin and Greek, he advocated mathematics and science. West Point, he believed, was the "only tolerable institution" in the land—"because of the absence there of the humbuggery of the learned languages." He hoped, too, that his physical survey would hasten the industrial development of Virginia and attract immigrants. The railroad development of Virginia rested largely on Maury's surveys. His colleague John Mercer Brooks, oceanographer and builder of the armament for the *Merrimac,* taught physics at V.M.I. until 1879, and before his death in 1906 had seen Maury's ideas of the New South in their full fruit.

Next door to V.M.I., with its scientific and military emphasis, lay the campus of Washington College, where Robert E. Lee, exponent of the New South, was president. There Congressman and Confederate Judge John White Brockenbrough became dean of the law school when he added his private law school to the college. It was Judge Brockenbrough, then a trustee of the struggling college, who had first crossed over the mountains to lay the cause of Washington College before General Lee. On Judge Brockenbrough's staff from 1870 to 1875 was John Randolph Tucker, attorney general of Confederate Virginia. Between 1875 and 1888 Tucker sat in Congress, battling valiantly against centralization, supporting sound money, opposing the protective tariff, and arguing the constitutional dogmas of states' rights. In 1888 he returned to Washington and Lee, became dean of the law school, and served until his death in 1897.

In 1894 Dean Tucker was president of the American Bar Association. He was the scholarly author of a standard study of constitutional law. He was, moreover, a skilled pleader for the principles of the Old South. Speaking to a graduating class of South Carolina College in 1887, he urged Carolinians to cling to Calhoun's philosophy and progress by rectitude and education. Only true principles, supported by moral strength, could enable the South to overcome the North's numerical preponderance. "No glory can come to the New South, and no real prosperity, if she repudiates the political philosophy of her ancestry, and abandons herself to the greed of gain." Dean Tucker was a startling example of the change which had come upon General Lee's institution.

During twenty-seven of the years of Dean Tucker's connection with Washington and Lee another Confederate major general, George Washington Custis Lee, was president. In February of 1871, a few months after his father's death, Custis Lee left V.M.I. to take over his father's office. The name of Washington College was changed to Washington and Lee University, and with another Lee—whose very name seemed to symbolize the institution—the college should have prospered. But Custis Lee, despite his heritage, his West Point training, and his experience as a teacher of engineering, was not equipped to carry on his father's tradition. He was a bachelor, shy and retiring from the public eye, yet an opinionated autocrat in matters academic. Much of the time he was ill, and frequently he begged the trustees to let him resign. Perhaps, like the son of Abraham Lincoln, he was overshadowed by his father's fame. Certainly, within a few years the number of students dropped alarmingly; the journalism scholarships were abandoned; the school of commerce, which had proposed to train the New South's leaders, declined; and academic standards dropped. After seven years with Custis Lee, Colonel William Preston Johnston, who had rescued Bishop Polk's plan from Bishop Quintard's "Domain" and made it a blueprint for General Lee's "University of the New South," resigned to go to Louisiana State. Only Judge Brockenbrough's old law school, housed in Tucker Hall, showed signs of vigor. It was training future politicians, lawyers, and jurists in the constitutional philosophy of John C. Calhoun.

Throughout the years between Appomattox and the end of the nineteenth century, while leading Confederates lent their talents to administering schools or instructing Southern youth, one among them stood pre-eminent as the evangel of education. Jabez Lamar Monroe Curry, a graduate of the University of

Georgia and the Harvard law school, was serving
his second term as congressman from Alabama when
his state seceded. He followed the state, went to the
provisional and first congresses of the Confederacy,
and was a lieutenant colonel of cavalry, serving on
the staffs of Generals Joseph E. Johnston and Joseph
Wheeler. At the close of the war he became, almost
simultaneously, a Baptist minister and an educator.
By the time of his death in 1903 he was the most
famous educational statesman of the South. He had
done more than any other individual to create a public
school system in the former Confederate States, had
established teacher-training schools in a dozen Southern states, had promoted rural education, had made
hundreds of addresses on educational subjects, had
written histories of the South, and had made volumi-
nous contributions to American educational literature.

He had begun as president of Howard College in
Alabama, and he remained there from 1865 to 1868.
Then he accepted the professorship of English, philosophy, and constitutional and international law at the
Baptists' Richmond College. For a time he added the
pastorship of the First Baptist Church in Richmond
and lectured and preached widely throughout the
country. In 1871 the University of Rochester gave
him a D.D. He spent the year between 1875 and 1876
in Europe. The next year his political disabilities were
removed, and President Rutherford B. Hayes offered
him a place in his cabinet. In 1881 he became agent

for the Peabody Fund and resigned from Richmond College. From 1885 to 1888 he was minister to Spain, resuming his work for the Peabody Fund on his return. In 1890 he became agent for the Slater Fund as well. In 1902 he was special ambassador to the coronation of Spain's Alfonso XIII. In the meantime, he wrote a *Civil History of the Confederacy*, a description of *The Southern States of the American Union*, a biography of *Gladstone*, studies of *Constitutional Government in Spain* and *Establishment and Dis-establishment in America*, dozens of magazine articles, and annual reports for the Peabody Fund. He served as president of the board of missions of the Southern Baptist Convention, of the board of trustees of Richmond College, and of the Southern Historical Society.

It was primarily as agent of the Peabody Fund that Curry contributed to Southern education. In 1867, George Foster Peabody, Massachusetts-born London merchant, gave one million dollars for "the promotion and encouragement of intellectual, moral and industrial education among the young of the more destitute portions of the Southern and Southwestern states." Two years later he added two million more— mostly northeastern railroad stock and the securities of Southern railroads, cities, and states. The first agent of the fund, Barnas Sears, president of Brown University, determined to use the money to aid local public-school agencies. Upon Sears's retirement,

Curry assumed control of the fund and directed it primarily to teacher-training. The John F. Slater Fund, a million-dollar gift of a Connecticut merchant, was for Negro education. After 1890 Curry administered both funds—using the Slater money to stimulate the training of teachers of manual arts and agriculture. Through these funds, and through the position as spokesman for education which they gave him, Curry became the key personality in the development of the public-school system in the South.

As spokesman and pundit, Curry's basic function was to compromise the philosophies of the Old and the New South. Between the thesis of those who lived by the words of "faith and reason"—Palmer and Pendleton and Bledsoe and Jones and the unbending Dabney—and their antithesis, who, living by the sword, had accepted the outcome of the ordeal by combat and joined Robert E. Lee and Stephen D. Lee and Roberts and Ross and Stewart and Maury in building a New South, Curry effected a synthesis containing elements of each.

The pattern for Curry's synthesis had been set, a generation before, by Horace Mann. While a student at Harvard, Curry had seen Mann persuading Massachusetts manufacturers that an educated people was a sure bulwark against social disorder and the best guarantee of stability in an industrial society. This was the concept that Curry carried to the South. He urged that education was essential for industrial prosperity, showing that Northern capital would not come south unless education insured order and trained the working class. He recognized the inferiority of the Negro and urged Southerners to provide training for the race that would make Negroes useful and skilled members of society. He reiterated the doctrines of states' rights, justified the Confederacy, and glorified the Confederate soldier. He fostered state-controlled schools which would teach "justice, right, honor and Christianity." He constantly assured the North that Southerners were loyal and patriotic. He justified white supremacy and separation of the races in the schools. In the South, he used his contact with the upper classes, with men of wealth, and with his fellow Confederate leaders to argue that education would preserve the best of the old traditions. In the end, he succeeded in fitting the philosophy of Jefferson Davis into the program of Robert E. Lee.

III.

Politics and Business:
The Leadership of Compromise

WHILE preachers and teachers—the spiritual
and intellectual leaders among the former
leaders of the Confederacy—divided their counsel on
the issues of the postwar decades, the political and economic leaders made practical adjustments to the new
order in Southern life. The process of rehabilitation
was, perhaps, simpler for educators and ministers
than for those who returned to the hustings or the
market place. For the former there were congrega-
tions waiting to hear an interpretation of the Word
or a newer generation eager to seize the power that
knowledge allegedly brought. But for those who depended upon governmental positions and for those
whose talents and ambitions ran to business, the immediate postwar situation offered frustrating obstacles. From the relative serenity of the classroom
and the pulpit, the men of words could indulge in theoretical speculations which weighed the relative
values of the Old South and the New. The men of
things, faced with the collapse of the old political system and of the old economic order, found it necessary

to compromise their avowed principles and to adjust their practices to a new world.

Neither politicians nor businessmen could afford an attitude of intransigence. While Jefferson Davis in his new role of political philosopher—aided by Bledsoe's pen and Palmer's preachings—clung to the doctrines of the Old South, he won few followers among the politicians and businessmen who had once been leaders of the Confederacy. They might, on the hustings, avow their undying devotion to the Lost Cause, and they might, in their relations with tenant farmers or mill hands, show a practical adherence to the principles of slavery; yet in substance they were followers of Robert E. Lee, men reconciled to the victory of the masters of capital and content to serve in the council chambers of their conquerors, and eager builders of a New South which acquiesced in its subservience to Northern countinghouses.

There were, of course, infinite variations on this central theme. There were extremes and compromises between extremes. There were rivalries, enmities, and suspicions among the leaders. There were conflicts between opposing interests and ambitions. But basic in the melee was the Southern Bourbons' effort, eventually effective, to show Northern capitalists that they —rather than the carpetbaggers, the scalawags, the Negroes, the Liberal Republicans, or the Readjusters —were the "safe" protectors of Northern interests. In the end, a New South emerged—a New South whose substance, if not its form, was symbolized by the "Compromise of 1877."

In the beginning, the prospect was dark indeed. For the politicians, the immediate outlook was clouded by the fact of their failure. The secession they had sponsored and the Confederacy they had directed had gone down to defeat. An occupying army stood, for a moment, in the place of state and local governments. Soon a program of presidential reconstruction would momentarily place political power in the hands of lesser politicos, who had hitherto been rejected by the people. Then a new military government, thrusting carpetbaggers into office and creating a new electorate, would hold sway. Through each successive regime the old leaders of the Confederacy labored to regain control. In the end, thanks in part to their own abilities and thanks in no small measure to the imbecility of their conquerors, the Confederate leaders rose again to be the trusted representatives of the Southern people. The 585 top military and civil leaders of the Confederacy furnished to the postwar South 418 holders of elective and appointive offices. Among them these 418 men held offices ranging from cabinet posts, senatorships, and foreign embassies to memberships on railroad and park commissions, postmasterships of cities, and even jobs as doorkeepers in the House of Representatives in the national government. In the states, they were governors, judges, legislators, members of constitutional conventions, sheriffs, councilmen, tax collectors, and court criers. But the very fact of their success is a measure of their compromise and a symbol of their surrender. Though their words might be the phrases of Davis, their acts were the deeds of Lee.

For businessmen among the Confederate leaders —and not all, by any count, of the Confederacy's first-ranking men were politicians—the first gloom after Appomattox seemed impenetrable. All but a scant handful of them were impoverished when their cause collapsed. Almost without exception they faced the immediate problem of making a living. Some had farms and plantations to which they might return to wrestle with the problems of raising crops without seeds, fertilizer, credit, or dependable labor. Some were lawyers who, like Virginia's Governor Letcher, could foresee fees in the litigation which would grow from the soil of chaos. But for the majority—and especially for the professional soldiers, whose trade was gone—there was only the immediate prospect of poverty. General P. G. T. Beauregard had exactly $1.15 in cash when he doffed his uniform. Lieutenant General R. H. Anderson worked as a day laborer in a railroad yard until he was recognized and made a station agent. Major General Matthew C. Butler returned to South Carolina with $1.75 in his pocket, $15,000 in debts, and a wife, 3 children and 70 former slaves to support.

Yet, in the years which followed, the qualities that had made these men leaders of the Confederacy made them in turn successful in business. Few among them died in poverty; many of them became wealthy. To the postwar South, the 585 top leaders of the Confederacy furnished 292 lawyers, 193 planters or farmers, 73 railroad officials, 39 merchants, 34 industrialists, 25 insurance men, and 23 bankers. Bringing to the test their prestige as Confederate leaders and their talents as executives, they led the way in the industrialization of the South. They were the embodiment of the principles of Robert E. Lee.

Not all, of course, of the Confederate leaders in politics and business were willing or able to compromise. A few, refusing to apply for amnesty or to cooperate with their conquerors, remained rebels at heart and in practice. In South Carolina, Judge Alfred P. Aldrich, who had worked ardently to secure secession and had been commissioner to persuade Missouri to follow the Palmetto State, was driven into recalcitrance by the military government. In 1865, in the Johnsonian constitutional convention, he voted against nullifying the ordinance of secession. Yet he had acquiesced in defeat, and had been elected to the circuit court. He was not long, however, in coming into conflict with the military government. In 1867 he sentenced a white man convicted of larceny to be whipped. The sentence did not accord with the local military commander's idea of justice, and he summoned Judge Aldrich to headquarters. When the judge refused to go, an officer arrived to escort him. When General Daniel E. Sickles upheld his subordinate, Judge Aldrich declared he could not hold court while his judgments, though strictly conforming to South Carolina law, could be summarily set aside by a military officer. Adjustments, however, were made, and the judge went back to his bench. But hardly had he resumed his duties when he received an order from General E. R. S. Canby to put Negroes on the jury lists. In open court the judge received the order and announced that he would not obey it. In a few days Canby ordered the judge suspended. Entering the church in Barnwell where he was holding court, Judge Aldrich read the order. "Gentlemen of the Juries," he said, "for the present, farewell. But if God spares my life I will yet preside in this court, a South Carolina Judge whose ermine is unstained. . . . Mr. Sheriff, let the court stand adjourned while the voice of justice is stifled." Taking off his gown, Judge Aldrich walked slowly from the church. True to his promise he came back. In 1878, after South Carolina was "redeemed," he was the only one of the old judges returned to the bench. During his retirement he was tireless in denouncing the usurpation of the military government, in addressing "taxpayers meetings," and in condemning Negro rule.

Even more uncompromising than Judge Aldrich

was Lieutenant General Jubal A. Early—the very embodiment of the "unreconstructed rebel." Although Early, a West Point graduate and a veteran of the Mexican War, had opposed secession in the Virginia convention, he entered the Confederate army as a colonel and rose to command a corps of Lee's army. Differing with Lee on the future course for Confederates, Early fled to Mexico—"to ascertain if there was any prospect of a war between Mexico and France on the one side, and the U.S. on the other, and to go into it, if there was." He hoped, too, to lead other Confederates to colonize the land. But he found Maximilian without support and vainly trying to win American approval. Thoroughly disappointed that Mexico "was no place for our people," Early went to Canada, where he vainly tried to find a means of livelihood.

He had, in those years, no desire to return to the United States until he could "participate in an effort to redeem our country, of which I do not despair." He saw no difference between Johnson and the radicals—both would bring the South to "abject humiliation." He hoped, in fact, that Thaddeus Stevens' plan would be put through—so the South would be provoked to revolution! He would not hear of reconciliation. No conquered people, he declared, ever "submitted with good will to the rule of their conquerors."

As Stevens' plan came into operation, and the South did not respond with revolution, the exile grew gloomy. He saw no new prosperity—as did the disciples of Lee—in railroad building. Railroads would only bring "increased burdens upon our people" and add to Virginia's impoverishment. The Congressional policy would unite the government under Negroes and "worthless whites."

But poverty drove General Early back to Virginia. Late in 1869, he hung out his defiant shingle in Lynchburg.

There, local legend recounted, he occupied an office in a building which was eventually condemned. Alone among the tenants, General Early refused to vacate. The workers came, razing all the building except the corner where Early had his office. Even the stairway was removed, but the general, who would not surrender to progress, mounted a ladder to his besieged den. Eventually, the general being absent, the wreckers pulled down the wall, and the office equipment tumbled into the rubble. Whatever the facts, the story had the truth which belongs to allegory.

No great success in the courts, General Early yielded to the blandishments of the Louisiana Lottery Company, who offered him a fabulous sum to serve, with General Beauregard, as "manager" of the lottery. Convinced that the drawings were honest, Early moved to New Orleans, where his name and prestige helped stay the demolition which that other unreconstructed rebel, the Reverend Doctor B. M. Palmer, demanded. When, eventually, Palmer's preachings combined with local political turmoil to demolish the lottery, General Early returned to Lynchburg.

Whatever prestige his association with the lottery may have cost him, the general more than made up by his work for the Southern Historical Society. At the inauguration of the society in 1873, Early became president, and until his death in 1894 he worked to advance its cause. He lectured widely, reminding Southerners again and again of the principles of the Lost Cause. He wrote, in addition to publishing his addresses on Civil War campaigns, a memoir of his own career. He had completed, by his death, a volume on *The Heritage of the South,* a historical justification of his own uncompromising stand.

Such intransigence as Early or Aldrich displayed was possible, at least in part, because neither of them was deeply involved in either politics or business. Other Confederates, too, remained unreconciled until their deaths, but most of these were farmers who were content to abandon active participation in public affairs or in expanding business. They tilled their fields, attended informal Confederate reunions on the verandas of country stores or formal ones at the county seat, and cherished the fading memories of their fugitive glory. They maintained their principles by abandoning the field.

How difficult it was for the unreconstructed rebel to remain without compromise was illustrated by the postwar career of Secretary of State Robert Toombs. The Georgia statesman had no reason to admire Jefferson Davis, yet as he began the postwar years, his truculence was somewhat akin to Davis' own spirit. Robert Toombs, selling part of his Texas lands to pay his way, went into exile in Cuba and Paris. From a safe distance he advised Southerners to avoid all cooperation with the victors. "The true policy of the South is to stand still, to do nothing," he told Vice-President Alexander H. Stephens. "Let the Yankees try their hand on Cuffee. If you try to help them all failures are yours, not theirs." He would not even support President Johnson. Returning home in the spring of 1867, he began to practice his precepts. He had an interview with Johnson—which ended with a tacit agreement that Toombs and the federal government would not molest one another. Though he had once been a United States senator, Toombs never applied for amnesty, never took part in national elections.

Yet even Toombs eventually succumbed to the new order. Upon his return he rebuilt his law practice, which eventually, with wise investment, made him wealthy. He took part in Georgia politics and served in the constitutional convention of 1877. In his early days he had been a conservative. In postwar Georgia, his opposition to corporations, products of the new Yankee spirit, almost made him a liberal. In the convention Toombs favored reducing the executive

patronage, shortening senatorial terms, and strength-
ening public control of corporations. He wanted railroads taxed, opposed unlimited franchises, and ob-
jected to state investment in railroad securities. Two
years later, he helped frame a bill for a state railroad
commission.

But wealth, success, and active concern in public
affairs brought reconstruction to Robert Toombs. He
began by fighting Joseph E. Brown, who advocated
collaboration with the victors. In the end Toombs and
Brown became reconciled. In 1872 Toombs opposed
the Democrats' fatuous endorsement of the Liberal
Republicans and Horace Greeley. In 1876 he opposed
Samuel J. Tilden as the Democratic choice—an attitude which made easier his endorsement of the bargain which gave Hayes the presidency. Though still
unpardoned, he was about to forgive. Eight years
later he gave complete approval to Grover Cleveland.
A year later, still technically unreconstructed, he died.

At the opposite extreme from Toombs and Early
and Aldrich stood a group of high-placed Confederates who rushed to embrace Republicanism and who
counseled collaboration with the Radicals. Some of
these, it is true, had never been Confederates at heart,
and merely resumed their Unionism after the war.
Brigadier General William C. Wickham had been
a Whig in the Virginia senate and a Unionist opposed
to secession in the secession convention. He raised a

cavalry company, gallantly led troops in battle, and returned to the war after each of several wounds. But in April of 1865, less than three weeks after Appomattox, he openly endorsed the Republican party as the "legitimate successor" of the Whigs. Before the year's end, he was president of the Virginia Central Railroad Company; and in three years, he was president of the Chesapeake and Ohio. Eventually he became receiver for the road. As an ardent Republican, he campaigned for Grant, refused President Hayes's offer of the post of secretary of the navy in his cabinet, and headed the Republican ticket for James A. Garfield in Virginia.

North Carolina had been a center of disaffection in the Confederacy, and many of her leaders embraced Republicanism without effort. Congressman James Graham Ramsey had been a Whig in North Carolina before the war. In the congressional elections of 1863 he stood on a peace program and went to Richmond as one of North Carolina's critical contingent to harass Jefferson Davis. It was no great shift for him to move over to the Republicans after the war. He returned to Rowan County to practice medicine and play at politics. He campaigned as an elector for Grant in 1872 and for Garfield in 1880, notwithstanding the ostracism which his neighbors accorded him. So, too, did another North Carolinian find the transition to Republicanism easy. Chief Justice Richmond Munford Pearson believed secession both immoral and unconstitutional. During the war, as a judge, he held conscription unconstitutional, and, as a politician, he gave his adherence to W. W. Holden. After the war he ran a law school in addition to serving as a provisional chief justice under Johnsonian reconstruction. Later, despite his Republicanism, he won the post at the polls and held office until his death in 1878. And North Carolina's Brigadier General Rufus Barringer, who had been a Whig and an opponent of secession but had led a cavalry unit for the Confederacy, came out of Fort Delaware, where he was a prisoner of war, early in 1865 to advise Tarheels to accept Negro suffrage. He endorsed Radical Republican dogmas and lent enthusiastic aid to the causes of temperance and industrial education.

Other states than North Carolina had furnished leaders to the Confederacy who had never been Confederates at heart. From Tennessee came George Earl Maney, originally an opponent of secession who, as a brigadier general, had followed Joseph E. Johnston to the end. After Greensboro, he returned to Murfreesboro and resumed his law practice. Within three years he was paper president of the paper Tennessee and Pacific Railroad and a quiet supporter of "Parson" Brownlow. In 1878 the Republicans nominated him for governor. He withdrew from the race but remained active in Republican politics. He campaigned for Garfield and for the next fifteen years reaped rewards as minister to a succession of Latin-

American governments. From Mississippi came James L. Alcorn, an Indiana-born Whig who opposed secession but served in the war as a brigadier general of state troops. In 1865 the Johnsonian government sent him to the United States Senate, where the Radical Republicans denied him a seat. He returned to Mississippi a Republican, however; served in the Radical constitutional convention of 1868; and became Republican governor the next year. From 1871 to 1877 he represented the carpetbag government in the United States Senate. But Alcorn showed more willingness to compromise than most scalawags. As governor he supported public education—with separate schools for the races—and as senator he resisted efforts to force Negro equality upon the South, denounced the federal cotton tax, and urged the removal of political disabilities from Southerners. This compromise did not secure his re-election, and he retired from office to make a fortune as a planter and merchant. From both Tennessee and Mississippi came Henry S. Foote, who had been Jefferson Davis' Unionist nemesis in Mississippi in the 1850's and who showed up in the Confederate Congress—his antipathy to Davis unchanged—as representative from Tennessee. After the war he practiced law in Washington, wrote anti-Southern histories, and wangled from Hayes an appointment as director of the New Orleans mint.

The Republicanism of these men who had been

Whigs, Unionists, and peace advocates was neither surprising nor inconsistent. Others, however, who joined the victors found it necessary to rationalize their course. Usually they set forth an argument based on expediency, advising their fellows to come to terms with their conquerors, "accept the situation," and look forward to the day when they might regain control.

Such was the course recommended by South Carolina's James L. Orr, an ardent champion of secession and a Confederate senator. At the end of the war he accepted presidential reconstruction and supported Johnson's provisional governor, B. F. Perry. Accompanying Perry to Washington on business, Orr balked at taking the steamer which would pass Fortress Monroe—he might soon be sent there, he said, and he had no desire to see the prison. In Washington, Orr begged President Johnson for a pardon. His willingness to accept the situation brought Orr election as governor, and his enthusiastic support of Johnson took him to the National Union Convention in Philadelphia in 1866. There Governor Orr won acclaim by leading the opening procession arm in arm with a general from Massachusetts. But Andrew Johnson lost the congressional elections that fall, and Governor Orr prepared to collaborate with the new victors. He had advised the rejection of the Fourteenth Amendment. Now he saw that reconstruction was inevitable and cast his influence towards extending the suffrage to Negroes. He co-operated with the military government, addressed the Radical "black and tan" convention, and announced his adherence to the Radicals. In 1868 he was elected a circuit judge, and on the bench he supported Grant's Ku-Klux policy. As he joined the Republicans, Orr told Perry that it was "important for our prominent men to identify themselves with the Radicals for the purpose of controlling their action and preventing mischief to the state." Although Perry thought that "if you join thieves you have to steal with them," he reported sorrowfully that "Judge Orr's notion of policy proved superior to all my notions of honor." But Orr's support of Grant's policy lost him the support which his good humor, cordial manners, and personal generosity had kept with him throughout his repeated adjustments to the changing political climate. Discredited at home, Orr accepted Grant's offer to be minister to Russia. In February of 1873, he arrived at his post to find seven feet of snow on Moscow's streets. In three months he was dead of pneumonia.

Two other exponents of the doctrine of expediency were Albert Gallatin Brown of Mississippi and Joseph E. Brown of Georgia. Mississippi's Brown had been among the most ardent of the Southern nationalists; as governor in the 1840's and as United States senator in the 1850's, he was far more radical in his Southernism than his fellow Mississippian Jefferson Davis. In the Confed-

erate Senate, he supported Davis' efforts to exercise
strong executive power. But once the war ended,
Brown was quick to abandon his principles for those
of Thaddeus Stevens. He urged Southerners to "meet
Congress on its own platform and shake hands." He
favored the Fifteenth Amendment, opposed partisan
sniping at President Grant, and advised welcoming
all immigrants "who come in good faith to share the
fortunes of the Southern people." His advice won him
no support, and he made no effort to solicit favors
from carpetbag governments or the federal administration. He died, poor and unsung, in 1880. He had
preached expediency but had not reaped its rewards.

Far different was the career of Joseph E. Brown,
Georgia's war governor. A vigorous personality,
skilled in political maneuvers and talented as a money-
maker, Governor Brown had been a states'-rights
thorn in President Davis' nationalist side. But, as he
told the Republican nominating convention in 1868,
"I had sense enough at the end of the struggle to
know when I was whipped." He was imprisoned for
a few days after the Confederacy's fall; but as soon
as he was released, he counseled the South to accept
reconstruction measures "as the quickest road to national rehabilitation." He followed his own advice
and quickly began to restore both his personal and
his political fortunes. In 1869, the scalawag governor Rufus B. Bullock appointed Brown chief justice
of Georgia. Within a few months Brown resigned to

become president of the Western and Atlantic Railroad, which he leased from the state. Within a few years Brown was a wealthy man, holding Atlanta real estate and serving as president of the Southern Railway and Steamship Company, the million-dollar Dade Coal Company, and the Walker Coal and Iron Company. He was part owner of the Rising Faun Iron Works. His riches enabled him to contribute heavily to the Baptist Church, the Southern Baptist Theological Seminary, and the University of Georgia.

In the meantime, Brown displayed a sense of the practical in politics as well as in economics. By 1880, his property safe and Republicanism no longer paying dividends, Brown returned to the Democratic party. In political alliance with Governor Alfred Colquitt and John Brown Gordon—"a triumvirate" dedicated to the cause of the commercial and industrial New South—Brown was boss of the state. Colquitt appointed him to the United States Senate when Gordon resigned to look after his own railroad interests. Re-elected, he served from 1880 to 1891.

But while the two Browns and Governor Orr were embracing Republicanism through expediency, and sundry Unionists and Whigs were passing naturally into the Republican party, it remained for Lieutenant General James A. Longstreet to formulate the principles of complete surrender. The last of Lee's associates to accept defeat in arms, counseling keeping up the fight to the last, Longstreet retired to civil life full of military honors and high-placed in Southern affections. Jobless and unprepared by West Point and his army career for civilian employment, he sought work. His name and fame took him to New Orleans as a partner in a cotton factorage and as head of an insurance business which paid him $5,000 a year. His business prospered so long as his grey uniform fitted snugly on his massive shoulders.

Early after the close of the war, Longstreet had, along with Lee and Beauregard, given expedient counsel. He had advised white Southerners to co-operate with the military authorities and save what they could from the situation. No one noticed his words nor heeded his advice—in fact, no one assumed that "Old Pete" had any especial convictions on the issues of the day. But early in 1867, as the Congressional Radicals passed the act dividing the South into military districts, General Longstreet announced himself in favor of the measure. After New Orleans had buzzed with excited disapproval for a couple of months, the editor of the *Times* called on Longstreet for a fuller exposition of his views. Readily the general complied. He wanted, he said, "practical reconstruction and reconciliation," and would be happy "to work in any harness that promises relief to our distressed people." Nor did it matter "whether I bear the mantle of Mr. Davis or the mantle of Mr. Sumner, so that I can bring the glory of peace and good will toward men."

With this introduction, Longstreet proceeded to a proposition that he held to be self-evident: "The highest of human laws is that established by appeal to arms!" The strongest laws "are those established by the sword." Since "the sword has decided in favor of the North," their principles "cease to be principles and become law. The views that we held cease to be principles because they are opposed to law. It is therefore our duty to abandon ideas that are obsolete and conform to the requirement of law."

Moreover, elaborating upon the theme, Longstreet explained that he had formerly acquiesced "in the ways of the Democracy, but, so far as I can judge, there is nothing tangible in them, beyond the issues that were put to the test in the war and there lost."

As a soldier who had lost both the war and his principles, General Longstreet saw Congress' Military Reconstruction Act as a "peace offering." If the Southerners would only accept the situation, "on to-morrow the sun will shine upon a happy people, our fields will again begin to yield their increase, our railroads and rivers will teem with abundant commerce, our towns and cities will resound with the tumult of trade, and we shall be invigorated by the blessings of Almighty God."

Longstreet was astounded at the public reaction to his views. The New Orleans *Times* denounced him as a traitor, men passed him on the street with averted eyes, and his business declined. Plaintively, the general appealed to President Lee of Washington College to endorse his views. But though Lee, too, had lived by the sword, and though he, too, looked forward to a happy, industrialized New South, he could not subscribe to Longstreet's program. Nor would Beauregard nor any other of the Confederate high command endorse the militarist doctrine that might makes right.

The only one of his old companions in arms who understood Pete Longstreet was Ulysses S. Grant, who was a companion from the old army. Longstreet and Grant were old friends; the Southerner had been best man at Grant's wedding. And at Appomattox, as the Union commander had left the conference with General Lee, he had locked arms with Longstreet: "Come on, Pete," he had said. "Let's play another game of brag." Now, as Confederates reviled Longstreet and spoke all manner of evil against him, and as his business failed, Grant came to his aid. One of his first acts as president was to appoint James A. Longstreet surveyor of the port of New Orleans.

Thereafter Longstreet was a partisan Republican, actively participating in the factional quarrels which marked Louisiana's turbulent politics. He supported the "Customs House Gang" that opposed Governor H. C. Warmoth and appealed to his old friend "Sam" Grant in behalf of Governor William Pitt Kellogg. When Grant recognized Kellogg and backed up his decision with federal troops, Kellogg made Longstreet adjutant of the state militia and levee commissioner at a salary of $6,000 a year. In September of 1874, when whites and Negroes clashed in New Orleans, it was Lieutenant General Longstreet of the Confederate army who led the Negro metropolitan police and the black state guard against White Leaguers whose ranks contained many a Confederate veteran.

Such partisanship brought a double reward. From successive Republican administrations, Longstreet received a succession of posts and honors. Hayes made him supervisor of internal revenue, postmaster of New Orleans, and minister to Turkey. Garfield made him United States marshal for Georgia. But former Confederate Longstreet reaped an opprobrium which cast a long shadow back over his military achievements. Shortly after Lee's death, General Pendleton charged that Longstreet's delay in obeying Lee's orders lost the battle of Gettysburg. Thereafter, to the end of his days, Longstreet was forced to defend his military as well as his political career.

Eventually the acrimony abated. Longstreet, aged forty-four when the war ended, lived forty more years. In time a new generation grew up in the South, and men felt less bitter on old controversies. Longstreet, too, became more moderate; and as his sight and hearing failed and his old throat wound from the Wilderness troubled him more and more, he grieved over his unpopularity in the land of his birth.

In 1896 and 1898 he received ovations from Confederate reunions. He was the last survivor of the Confederate high command, and old men remembered best the scenes of their youth. Old men who had forgotten much and young men who had never known mellowed and forgave the soldier who had surrendered most.

But those who joined the Republicans through predilection, expediency, or principle were but a scant minority among the onetime leaders of the Confederacy. So, too, were those who took an intransigent stand on the principles of the Old South. The great majority of Confederate leaders who went into business or into politics bent an expedient knee to circumstance and sought a formula for a compromise which would accommodate the practices of the victorious North to the mores of the Old South. Although the formula was difficult, and they remained in the Democratic party and gave verbal adherence to the principles of the Lost Cause, they, too, were collaborators with their conquerors.

Almost three hundred of the Confederacy's leading men returned to the practice of law after Appomattox. For the most part, of course, they practiced politics as well; and scores of them sat in Congress, in state legislatures, or in constitutional conventions, occupied governors' mansions, or adorned the bench. But almost without exception those who

achieved prominence in the postwar South were corporation lawyers—serving as counsel, as directors, or
as presidents of railroads, mining companies, or manufacturing establishments.

Thus, John Cabell Breckinridge, onetime vice-
president of the United States and major general and
briefly secretary of war in the Confederacy, returned
to his native Kentucky in 1869 after a period as
refugee in Cuba, Europe, and Canada. He received
an ovation in Lexington on the night of his return;
but when his welcoming neighbors offered him their
support for public office, he told them he was done
with politics. Instead, he assumed the lead in his
state's economic development. Kentucky, like the Confederate states, offered a fertile field for Northern
economic exploitation. Breckinridge's popularity was
great, and he immediately received offers of employment. He chose railroads, which had interested him
even before the war. He became a promoter and stock-
holder of the Elizabethton, Lexington, and Big Sandy
Railroad Company—a vital link between Louisville
and the Atlantic seaboard and potentially the only
east-west road in the state. At the same time he became counsel for the Cincinnati Southern Railroad
and began a long battle to obtain a right of way across
the state. The battle was hard fought, for the road
which would connect Cincinnati with Chattanooga
conflicted with business interests in the city of Louisville. Only the popularity of Breckinridge could over-

come the local opposition to granting favors to a foreign corporation. Before the legislature Breckinridge lobbied diligently against Louisville. When Louisville spent $4,000 entertaining the legislators at the ceremonial opening of an Ohio River bridge, Breckinridge induced the legislators to visit Cincinnati, where the Ohioans spent $6,000 entertaining them. Buchanan's vice-president spent $20,000 in his lobbying activities and received $3,000 for his services. Before a committee of the legislature he declared that the Cincinnati road would introduce ten million dollars in capital into the state, making Kentucky "great, strong, and prosperous." The whole state would prosper—yea, the whole South, and even the nation. The railroad would unite in "free social and commercial intercourse" the divided sections. In 1872 success crowned his efforts. Meantime, Breckinridge became vice-president of the Elizabethton, Lexington, and Big Sandy road—an important link in Collis P. Huntington's Chesapeake and Ohio line—and counsel and lobbyist for the C. and O. as well. Before ill health suddenly stopped his activities, he was well on the way to a fortune. Yet by the time of his death in 1875, he had made a distinctive contribution to opening Kentucky to the economic penetration of Northern capital.

Other ex-Confederate leaders throughout the South followed Breckinridge's course. Speaker of the Confederate House of Representatives Thomas

S. Bocock was attorney for three railroads in Virginia; Kentucky's congressman in Richmond, Horatio W. Bruce, after a term on the bench, resigned in 1880 to become attorney for the Louisville and Nashville Railroad. Arkansas' Brigadier General William L. Cabell moved to Dallas and became mayor, and vice-president and general manager of the Texas Trunk Railroad. Tennessee's Brigadier General Alexander W. Campbell returned to Jackson to be president of the Bank of Madison and to hold directorships in the Mobile and Ohio Railroad and the Northern-owned Jackson Gas-Light Company. Virginia's Congressman Charles F. Collier was president of the Petersburg and Weldon Railroad from 1868 to 1872. North Carolina's Brigadier General William R. Cox was United States congressman and senator, a judge, and an orator who extolled the Southerners as the purest type of the Anglo-Saxon race. In addition he was president of the Chatham and Coldfield Railroad and a director of the National Bank of Raleigh. Brigadier General Basil Duke returned to Kentucky and went into the legislature, where he sponsored laws regulating railroads. Then he took a position as counsel for the Louisville and Nashville and spent twenty years battling for the company against the state's regulatory laws. Mississippi's Congressman Jehu Amaziah Orr lived on until 1921, lecturing on "The Bible as a Textbook for

Lawyers and Statesmen," serving as judge, and practicing law as a railroad attorney and promoter. And
Assistant Secretary of War Robert Ould, who had
been Confederate agent for the exchange of prisoners
and an irascible advocate on obscure points of international law against agents of the Northern prison
administration, settled in Richmond to write theological tracts, practice railroad law, and serve as
president of a publishing company. Tennessee's Congressman Arthur S. Colyar was president of the Tennessee Coal and Iron Company before settling down
to a career as editor and publisher in Nashville.

But perhaps the career of Tennessee's John Calvin Brown most fully illustrated the case of the lawyer
turned industrial builder of the New South. A zealous
Whig before the war and an opponent of secession,
Brown entered the Confederate army a private and
came out a major general. After being wounded in
the battle of Franklin, he resumed his law practice in
Pulaski; and immediately after the war, he became
president of the Nashville Railroad Company. He
was no supporter of Governor Brownlow in politics,
but he differed not at all from the "Parson" in his
eagerness to promote Tennessee's industrialization.
In 1870 he was chairman of the constitutional convention, and later in the year he accepted the label of
"Democrat" and ran for governor. His rival for the
Democratic nomination, A. S. Colyar, was less inter-

ested in election than in advancing the principles of industrialism and dropped out of the race in Brown's favor.

As governor of Tennessee from 1871 to 1875, Brown devoted his efforts to building prosperity. In 1873 he urged the legislature to support the state bureau of agriculture and worked diligently to persuade the legislators to fund, consolidate, and regularize the payment of the state's thirty-million-dollar debt. He was especially solicitous that the state's railroad bonds should be paid. He was, moreover, eager to encourage railroad building and immigration.

Industrial development intrigued the governor, and he spent much time in studying means "to bring to the attention of the world our vast, undeveloped Iron and Coal fields." The future greatness and prosperity of Tennessee, he fervently proclaimed, depended upon "how . . . this hidden wealth, piled up with nature's lavish hand, [is] to be developed and utilized." There was, he ruefully admitted, surplus capital at home, "but our people are sadly deficient in enterprise and confidence." Tennesee's own capitalists preferred to invest their money in bonds rather than to take the risk of enterprises which would, if well managed, enrich both them and the state. "There is, in the city of Nashville, enough of Capital held in that way to make a respectable Pittsburgh of the city." But Brown despaired of Tennessee's capitalists. "We must look abroad," he announced, to attract Pennsyl-

vania iron men and English miners and manufacturers, and persuade them that Tennessee's iron
would yield a larger return than that of other re-
gions. Moreover, the laws should protect the outside
investor. When race riots came in Memphis in 1874,
Governor Brown took prompt steps to suppress disorder and protested against federal interference. In-
vestors in Tennessee had to be shown that the state
had vigor and strength and the will to establish and
maintain order.

After his term as governor, Brown continued his
work of bringing capitalists to the South. Thomas
A. Scott, president and builder of the Pennsylvania
Railroad, was pushing the development of the Texas
and Pacific Railway. Scott, who had managed transportation for the federal War Department during
the Civil War, realized the need for a Southern ally
of intelligence, diligence, and integrity. He offered
Brown a position as counsel for the road, and Brown
enthusiastically embraced the opportunity. He lobbied for the T. and P. before the Texas legislature
and before Congress; he pleaded the cause of the
Yankee-owned road before chambers of commerce
and boards of aldermen in St. Louis, Memphis, and
New Orleans. His enthusiasm and his apparent integrity won confidence, and his cause prospered. In
1880, Jay Gould took over the Southern Pacific Lines,
and Brown became general solicitor of the Gould
roads west of the Mississippi—the Missouri Pacific,

the Missouri, Kansas, and Texas, the Iron Mountain, the Texas and Pacific, the New Orleans and Pacific, and the Great Northern Railroad. For these lines Brown lobbied before the legislatures and argued in the courts of Missouri, Kansas, Texas, Louisiana, and the Indian Territory. In 1885, Brown became receiver of the bankrupt Texas and Pacific Railroad. While it was in his hands, he practically rebuilt the line; and in 1888, upon its reorganization and discharge from receivership, Brown became president of the road.

But his health suffered from his labors. He petitioned his employers to return him to Tennessee. Grateful for his services, they made him president of the Tennessee Coal and Iron Company, the South's largest industrial corporation. But within a year Brown's heart failed. A marble statue, life-size, marks his grave in the Pulaski cemetery. Clad in Confederate uniform, with his hand upon his sword and his gaze toward the South, the stylized figure fails to convey the significance of John Calvin Brown as a builder of the New South.

Other Confederate leaders besides those who practiced law were intimately connected with Southern railroads. Altogether, more than seventy top-ranking Confederates found employment and opportunity and wealth in the railroads which sprang up in the South after Appomattox. Army officers, lacking talent and experience for other business, could turn their West Point training into use in railroad engineering. Thus, General Braxton Bragg, refurbishing his engineering lore, moved to New Orleans as superintendent of the waterworks there and then to Mobile to be a civil engineer supervising harbor improvements. After four years as commissioner of public works for the state of Alabama, he became chief engineer of the Gulf, Colorado, and Santa Fe Railroad. Later, until his death in 1875, the state of Texas employed him to inspect the railroads built with the state's land subsidies. Thus, too, General Beauregard, finding his Louisiana plantation unable to support him, and successively failing to get employment in the armies of Brazil, Rumania, or France, accepted the presidency of the New Orleans, Jackson, and Great Northern Railroad and later of the Carrollton Railroad. He traveled to Europe, seeking funds for the Jackson road. By his own confession he found the work "congenial and natural" and preened himself for having become "quite a railroad man." But when the Illinois Central acquired the Jackson road, Beauregard lost his job. Thereafter he tried to get a military post in Argentina and almost entered the Egyptian service. Eventually, all these efforts failing, he accepted the nominal management, along with General Early, of the Louisiana Lottery. He spent his last days, until his death in 1893, alternately defending his military record against the disparagement of Jefferson Davis and defending the lottery against the assaults of the moralists.

Other Confederate leaders who bartered their prestige for railroad positions or sold their engineering or managerial skills to railroad corporations included Brigadier General Edward Porter Alexander, who, after being professor of engineering at the University of South Carolina, entered railroading to become president of the Georgia Railroad and Banking Company and, eventually, a government director of the Union Pacific. There was North Carolina's Congressman Robert R. Bridgers, who was twenty times re-elected president of the Wilmington and Weldon Railroad and helped to build up the Atlantic Coast Line. South Carolina's Brigadier General James Conner was solicitor for the South Carolina Railroad Company and receiver for the Greenville and Columbia. Brigadier General John Echols, of Staunton, Virginia, aided in reorganizing the Chesapeake and Ohio and served for twenty years as a director of the road. North Carolina's Brigadier General William McRae was successively general superintendent of the Wilmington and Manchester, the Macon and Brunswick, and the Georgia State Road. Virginia's Major General William Mahone had the unique distinction of having been a railroad president before the war. After the war he returned to railroading and joined three lines into the Atlantic, Mississippi, and

Ohio Railroad. He took an active part, for the benefit of his line, in Virginia's reconstruction politics. He
lost his road in the crash of 1873 but continued his
political causes. He organized the Readjuster movement in Virginia, went to the United States Senate,
and became the head of the Republican machine in
the Old Dominion.

Greatest of the ex-Confederates who turned railroad men was Thomas M. Logan, a South Carolinian
who became a brigadier general at the age of twenty-
four. During the war, he met the daughter of the
owner and manager of the Clover Hills Mines near
Petersburg. Within a month after Appomattox he
married her and began to assist his father-in-law in
managing the mines and a spur-line railroad which
ran to them. At the same time, Logan completed law
studies he had begun during the war. In 1866 he
moved to Richmond to open a law office, and the
next year he became president of the railroad to the
Clover Hills Mines.

This modest beginning launched Logan on a railroad career which boomed steadily until his death in
1914. About 1878 Logan began to buy stocks in the
Richmond and Danville Railroad. Soon he headed a
syndicate which operated a terminal company which,
in turn, owned stocks in other railroads. He built the
Georgia and Pacific Railroad from Birmingham to
the Mississippi and, acquiring other lines, became engaged in consolidating the Southern system. He

weathered a bear attack in Wall Street and emerged as a partner in railroad deals with John D. Rockefeller. He bought the Seattle, Lake Shore and Eastern Railroad and sold it for a profit to the Northern Pacific. He served from 1888 to 1914 as president of the Gray Telautograph Company.

In addition to his superlative talents as a railroad builder, Logan was an exceptionally articulate advocate of a new, industrialized South. Early in his Richmond career, he began writing articles for the Richmond *Enquirer,* the Manchester *Courier,* and other papers. In them and in numerous addresses he preached the doctrines of industrialization, the virtues of hard work, and the gospel of the railroads. "We regard it as a good sign that in the depressed condition of life in the South the railroad interest seems to be the most active and progressive one at present," he declared in an early article. And, he added, "the fact that this is due to Northern capital is by no means discouraging." It was, he thought, only folly to complain that the roads would be controlled by Northern capital. In 1876, writing in *Harper's Monthly,* he boasted of the South's growing industrialization. "It is time," he proclaimed, "that childish despondency makes way for manly energy . . . that vain lamentations over the past yield to hopeful anticipations of the future." And the next year, addressing a reunion of Texas veterans, he called for the nationalization of America and the strengthen-

ing of federal authority. A few months later, Logan
spoke to the American Social Science Association on
Negro education. Public education for the black
would make him less prone to manipulation by dema-
gogues—"when taught to read he is brought within
the influence of the Press."

In politics Logan was a gold Democrat, a follower
of Cleveland, and an opponent of Populism and
Bryanism. By word and deed he taught the South to
abandon its old ways for the mores of its conquerors.
By precept and practice he taught Northern businessmen that Southern leadership could be trusted to manage Southern property for the benefit of Northern
owners.

Although railroads possessed a peculiar glamor for
men of the late nineteenth century and absorbed the
energies of many of the Confederacy's former leaders,
industry and finance enlisted other ex-Confederates.
Almost sixty of the top-ranking Confederates found
postwar employment and opportunity for wealth in
mines and mills and banks and blast furnaces; and almost without exception they served, as did the railroad men, as managers of Northern-owned property.
Some, like Brigadier General John D. Imboden, who
was general superintendent of the National Express
Company, became propagandists encouraging foreign capital to come south to exploit the section's natural resources. Imboden's *Coal and Iron Resources*

of Virginia, published in 1872, became a veritable guidebook for Northern adventurers seeking mineral wealth. Some, like Major General Matthew C. Butler, combined an active political career with sundry financial and industrial adventures. He was a South Carolina state legislator in 1865, an unsuccessful candidate for lieutenant governor of the Union Reform Convention in 1870, a United States senator from 1877 to 1895, and a major general of volunteers in the Spanish-American War. In addition he practiced law at Edgefield, South Carolina, and Washington, D.C., formed the corporation which bought South Carolina's stock in the Blue Ridge Railroad in 1871, promoted a lottery company which planned to settle immigrants on Southern lands, supported the Blue Ridge Canal Company, and was president of the Mexican Mining and Exploration Company. Others became industrialists or financial agents of Northern capital through natural drift. Alabama's Confederate Congressman David Clopton combined duties as an associate justice of the state supreme court with directorships in Sheffield's First National Bank and the Sheffield Coal and Iron Company. Alabama's Brigadier General Birkett Davenport Fry, whom General Bragg cryptically described as a man of "gunpowder reputation," first fled to Cuba, then returned to Tallassee, Alabama, to manage a cotton mill, moved in 1881 to Richmond as a cotton buyer, managed a cotton mill, and from 1886 to his death in 1891 was president of the Northern-controlled Marshall Manufacturing Company. Major General Robert F. Hoke had been engaged in manufacturing before the war, managing a cotton business and even establishing a cottonseed-oil mill. At the close of the war he bade touching farewell to his troops, urging them to cherish "the love of liberty which led you into the contest." He set an example to his men by going into the field and making a crop with his war horse. But soon he was prospecting for gold in the North Carolina mountains. He found iron in the Cranberry district and formed the Chapel Hill Iron Mine and the Cranberry Iron Mine. Both of these he owned, in large part; but his railroad interests made him eventually a manager of Northern capital. He was president of the Georgia, Carolina, and Northern Railroad Company and of the Seaboard Airline.

The drift towards Northern capital was well illustrated in the postwar career of Brigadier General Thomas Taylor Munford, a graduate of V.M.I. and a planter in Bedford, Virginia, before the war. Thomas Munford's father, George Wythe Munford, was secretary of the Commonwealth of Virginia before and during the war. The family was well connected, being related to the Tuckers, prominent in the law and in the Episcopal Church, and to Charles Ellis, president of the Richmond and Petersburg Railroad. At the close of the war, General Munford returned to his Bedford farm, while his father, selling his house in Richmond, rented a farm for $1,600 a year.

As a farmer, neither father nor son was successful. The elder Munford began with enthusiasm, which quickly declined as he faced the problem of getting work out of his Negro employees. "I have reached 63 years and am just in the full tide of the experiment whether I can compete with Cuffee as a day laborer or not," he explained to Ellis. He described his carriage: "Alas, you ought to see it. The once upon a time Secretary of the Commonwealth of Virginia and candidate for the Governorship of the Old Dominion, driving up to church with a family who would grace the gubernatorial mansion in a wagon drawn by three mules couldn't even drive four in hand." Yet, he concluded, if he could get started, he would prefer a farmer's life to "delving for the public at the Capitol." But the start never came: his Negroes wouldn't work, his notes fell due, his crops would not sell. He borrowed from his son and from Ellis. Eventually he abandoned his rented farm to buy a smaller one, but within a couple of years he had become totally dejected. "If I had the capital to continue my improvements a year or two longer," he told his son in 1869, "I believe I could then make a support, but my resources have all been exhausted and I do not see what I can do other than to sell out and still reduce down, down to a lower state, and come to the level at once of the lower classes, face the music, and live as they do." Finally, Munford began soliciting help from Richmond. He got a job as clerk for a legislative committee and then a windfall of $5,000 for revising the code of Virginia. In 1872, through his son's influence, Munford became secretary of the Southern Historical Society at $2,500 a year. But this did not pay either, and Munford got a place as an auditor. In 1880, the Readjusters turned him out of the place, and Beverly Tucker and General Joseph E. Johnston persuaded President Hayes to give the aged man a berth in the Census Bureau at a stipend of $1,000 per year.

In the meantime, General T. T. Munford was struggling valiantly against following his father's fate. He returned penniless to his farm to find his implements gone and his laborers worthless. But "Thom" Munford was, as his father said, "rather fond of speculation." He bought cattle—180 head for $8,000—and drove them to Richmond and Baltimore for sale. The next year he planned to develop a dairy farm employing only white laborers, and he went to New York to select stock and study the dairy industry. He had, said his wife, "cheese on the brain"; but the general assured his father that he had "demonstrated the fact that a cow will yield nearer $100 than $60 a year in cheese." Moreover, he was buying lean sheep culled from dealers' droves, fattening them, and reaping profits from wool, lambs, and mutton. But all these projects—and even a venture into pea culture—failed to lift the burden of debt from him. "I am disgusted with farming," he told his father. "I work hard all year, pay the negroes every cent I can get my hands on, and have nothing to credit myself and farm with. My wheat brought me in debt. . . ."

But luck came to the aid of Thom Munford: his father-in-law in Alabama died, and Thom took over the estate. He acquired cotton lands in Alabama and city property in Massachusetts. Moreover, his new property gave him an opportunity to indulge his fondness for speculation. A neighbor had invented "a forced air water-pump for lifting water from a spring or deepwell to the 3rd. or 4th. story of a house," and Munford bought "an interest in it for the Middle and Southern States." It would, he thought, be "of great value to the country people." But soon he expanded his plan, enlisted the services of two engineering professors at the Virginia Military Institute, and proposed to supply the city of Lynchburg with water.

The panic of 1873 and the political disturbances in the South delayed the launching of the pump company. Both Munfords deplored the Radical excesses. The elder supported the conservative party in Virginia. "It is vastly important," he believed, "to keep the government in the hands of the whites." When Thom complained of financial embarrassment, George Wythe Munford assured him that the times were generally hard: "The South with bad crops and bad government has had woeful times and as long as radical rule prevails they will see harder times yet." Thom, however, thought that Virginia was certainly better off than Louisiana—"those people with Sheridan riding over them. If the Devil don't get him *he* certainly will not get *all* his dues—and if there is not a Brutus in N. Orleans the people are changed indeed." Both Munfords found the federal government's policies injurious in other respects. The father thought there was not enough money in circulation—and "there never will be a stable currency until the government forces a resumption of specie payments." The son thought it impossible for a Southern farmer to make money in competition with the free lands of the West. The father spoke venomously before Richmond's Konservative Kampaign Klub,and the son denounced Alabama's Radical congressmen who stirred up the "intimidated" Negroes.

But hope revived with a return of stability and some conservative successes in elections. By 1874 Thom thought the political condition of Alabama was "decidedly improved." Early the next year he organized his Pneumatic Pump Company in Lynchburg and had advance orders for twenty-three pumps. Two years later, he helped organize the Clifton Forge and Buchanan Railroad; this, he hoped, would give work to the "iron and car shops" which he owned. By 1880, at the time his father moved to Washington to labor for a pittance in the Census Bureau, General T. T. Munford had turned over the management of his

Alabama plantations to his son and was concentrating his attention on his Lynchburg ironworks. He was vice-president of the Lynchburg Iron, Steel, and Mining Company, dealing generally in machinery, bridges, railroad supplies, hydraulic presses, and iron ore. He was out of debt; but, as he explained to his mother, he had been "in a very sad way until the 'boom' came" and the company was formed. By that time, too, Thom was in league with Philadelphia iron interests. As his aged father bent over a Census Bureau desk under the supervision of a librarian—"a copper colored darkey," reported a relative—Thom was actively promoting a banquet for "40 eastern men— capitalists from Pennsylvania and New York looking for iron and steel manufacturing locations." "Capital and energy" were all that Lynchburg needed, he announced, "to be more prosperous than Penna." Thereafter, until his death in 1918, General Thomas Taylor Munford pursued two avocations: the military history of the Confederacy and the industrialization of Lynchburg.

In the meantime, throughout these years when Munford and Logan and John C. Brown and a myriad of others were struggling to build the railroads, the iron mines, the blast furnaces, and the cotton mills of the New South—at first with local capital and then, in desperation, with Northern aid—the victorious Northern masters of capital, tycoons of industry, and lords of the countinghouses had been trying a succession of experiments to gain control of Southern wealth. The political agents of these men were the Radical members of the Republican party. During the Civil War, Radical congressmen, capitalizing upon the moral and humanitarian sentiments of the Northern people and bending to their use the propaganda and preachings of the abolitionists, had wrought momentous changes in the national economy. They had raised the tariff to heights beyond the wildest dreams of the most ardent disciple of Alexander Hamilton. They had made the national debt, which Hamilton had declared a national blessing, into a permanent base for a national banking system. They had subsidized internal improvements by handing over great portions of the nation's wealth and resources to the builders of railroads. These were the "results of the war" so far as the masters of capital were concerned; and these "results" they hoped to secure, perpetuate, and improve by the measures of the reconstruction decade.

But there were other "results" which the victorious masters of capital hoped to obtain through the war and reconstruction. Before and during the war Northern merchants and manufacturers and financiers had looked upon the South as a potential market for their goods and services. The South offered a prospective field for Northern investments; its lands might be colonized by immigrants subsidized from the

North; its mines and transportation systems and mill sites and harbors might be made to bring profits into Northern coffers. All this, of course, was an acquisitive dream, but the dream of securing these "results" as well made up the second phase of reconstruction.

As the political agents of the masters of capital, the Radical Republicans made, in substance, a dual promise: to prevent the old Southern leaders from regaining the power to threaten the "results of the war," and to make easy the road for Northern economic penetration and exploitation in the South. Their attempts to fulfill their promises produced the disturbances of reconstruction. They began by rejecting President Johnson's provisional governments and refusing seats in Congress to Southern representatives. Then they extended the Freedmen's Bureau and drafted the Fourteenth Amendment to the Constitution. Meeting resistance, they resorted to military government and to army-backed governments of carpetbaggers and scalawags resting upon a controlled electorate composed of enfranchised freedmen.

In the long run, none of these devices proved effective means for exploiting the South. Passive resistance—passive at least to the extent that there was no unified armed uprising—and underground opposition defeated the purposes of the Radicals. There was no Brutus, as Munford had hoped there would be, in New Orleans to deal with the tyrant Philip H.

Sheridan, but neither was there effective collaboration. The collaborationist Longstreet had few imitators and no followers. Moreover, the Radical system of government by army officers, carpetbaggers, scalawags, and Negroes did not promote the order and quiet that business needed before it would venture into the region. And at the same time the national government was falling into corruption; scandals marked the presidency of Ulysses S. Grant, and declining confidence in the government contributed to the panic of 1873. Disorder in the South and discontent in the North eventually brought Northern businessmen to the point of abandoning the attempt to reconstruct the South.

In the meantime, the Munfords and Logans and Browns—to say nothing of Generals Simon Buckner and Joseph E. Johnston and Gustavus W. Smith, who had gone into the insurance business as agents of Northern companies—were striving to build a New South upon the Northern model. They scorned the Radical party, rejected Negro suffrage, and repudiated the political collaborationists among them. They gloried in their history and made no verbal admission that the South had been wrong in secession. But their deeds, at long last, spoke louder than their words. One by one they "redeemed" their states, administered them with conservatism and economy, and established order. They made bids for Northern capital. And at long last the masters of capital understood that the deeds of Lee were more potent than the words of Davis.

The outward and visible symbol of this understanding was the "Compromise of 1877." In that year, Southerners agreed to acquiesce in the dubious settlement which placed Rutherford B. Hayes in the White House instead of Democrat Samuel J. Tilden. But they understood that the price of their acquiescence was the withdrawal of federal troops from the South. Hayes fulfilled the unwritten bargain; and as the troops left the South, the last of the Southern states fell into the hands of the conservative Southerners, the Southern Republican party collapsed, and the solid South began.

But there was a deeper reality hidden behind this outward symbol. The settlement was unwritten and unformulated; but it was, in fact, the last sectional compromise in a long series which had begun with the three-fifths compromise in the Philadelphia Convention and had run through the Missouri Compromise, the Nullification Compromise of 1833, and the Compromise of 1850. The "Compromise of 1877" never bore the once-honored name of "compromise"; but it was, in its lasting effects, the greatest of them all. Perhaps, indeed, it was the greater and more lasting solely because it was unwritten.

The settlement which might well have been designated the "Compromise of 1877" transcended mere political arrangements to deal with more substantial matters. In its essence it left local government and local social arrangements in the South in the hands of Southerners. No longer—except for Northern political consumption—would Yankee politicos agitate the Negro question. The Negro's destiny, at least in the South, rested in the hands of the Southern whites. Northerners, having freed the Negro as a chattel and used him as a political instrument, abandoned him to his servitude in a system. But, in addition to politics and race, the "Compromise" contained economic understandings. Northern interests would take over the mines and the mills, the railroads and the banks of Dixie; but Southerners—the onetime leaders of the Confederacy and the newer generation rising to take their places—would manage the property. Confederate leaders were to be presidents of Northern-owned railroads, directors of Yankee-dominated corporations, superintendents of Northern-financed factories. The division of labor would be complete. The Southerners would receive the rewards of management— local prestige, good salaries, local offices—and the Northerners would reap the profits of ownership. Thus, through an alliance with the proponents of the New South, would the masters of Northern capital penetrate the South and realize the dream which Radical reconstruction had failed to fulfill.

The settlement, however, did not endanger by any means the perpetuation of the system which meant, to the masters of capital, the "results of the war." The protective tariff, the national banking system, the grants to railroads, and all the other war-borne gifts to the disciples of Alexander Hamilton and Henry Clay remained secure. Through the years, high-ranking Confederates sat in the legislative halls of their conquerors; but, with few exceptions, they displayed no serious disposition to disturb the economic results of the war.

Seventy-three of the highest-placed Confederates sat, at one time or other, in the United States Senate or House of Representatives. Together with the other ex-Confederates they bore the collective sobriquet "rebel brigadiers" and were popularly ridiculed for their conservative votes and general quietness. Occasionally some ambitious politician succeeded in baiting a Southerner to rise to indignant defense of Southern honor, as James G. Blaine trapped Georgia's Senator Benjamin H. Hill into defending Andersonville Prison; but, for the most part, the rebel brigadiers raised no rebel yell and gave few exhibitions of the South's famed oratory. Without exception, they were Democrats, voting ineffectively with their party for tariff reduction, against internal improvements, for the gold standard, and for economy. But never did they constitute a Confederate bloc in either Congress or the Democratic party.

Instead of an arrogant or recalcitrant Southernism, the ex-Confederate leaders were prone to seize opportunities to proclaim their Unionism. Thus in 1874, the onetime Confederate diplomat L. Q. C. Lamar sprang to the occasion to deliver in the House a eulogy of Charles Sumner. Four years later Confederate Vice-President Alexander H. Stephens, now a congressman from Georgia, used the presentation of F. B. Carpenter's pictured "Emancipation Proclamation" as excuse to enjoin "forbearance" and the "conquering of prejudices" upon his fellow congressmen. And Benjamin H. Hill, senator from Georgia in the Confederate and United States Congresses, supported the bill to restore ex-President U. S. Grant to his rank as general of the army. As a veteran of the Confederate army expressed it in 1878 to Blaine, "The people of the North and South want rest from political agitation. Business relations, business interests, and business success can grow only when such rest is given them." Carefully the Confederate advised Northerners to "arouse the cupidity of their [Southern] leaders by aiding them in material progress and internal development." If the South's highways were reopened, Northern manufacturers would find a market. "May we not recognize the fact that political reconstruction has failed of its primary purpose, but that business reconstruction and material progress are the aims of the South and the interest of the North."

For long years the galaxy of Confederate stars in the national legislature included such men as Confederate Postmaster General John H. Reagan of Texas, who distinguished himself by continuous insistence on railroad regulation; North Carolina's war governor Zebulon B. Vance, who sat in the Senate as a consistent opponent of civil service reform and a high tariff; and Missouri's George Vest, who served two years in the Confederate Senate and twenty-four years in the United States Senate and fought tariff increases, the Blair Education Bill, railroad subsidies, and all modern improvements, but who was best known for his famed tribute to "Man's Best Friend, the Dog."

But perhaps the congressman who best represented the conciliatory spirit was "Fighting Joe" Wheeler, the lieutenant general of cavalry who fought two hundred battles and eight hundred skirmishes during the Civil War. Shortly after the war General Wheeler, scarcely thirty years of age, went to New Orleans as a commission merchant. A few years later, his newly acquired father-in-law induced the cavalry leader to take up farming in Alabama. In Lawrence County, Wheeler raised cotton and, getting admitted to the bar, practiced law. Both activities were profitable, and Wheeler invested his profits in railroad securities. By 1880, the onetime general was attorney for the East Tennessee, Virginia, and Georgia Railroad Company and a member of its board of directors. Completely identified with the New South philosophy, Wheeler entered politics as a Bourbon and a conservative opponent of an agrarian "Independent" faction of Alabama politics. On the issue of "white supremacy," Fighting Joe Wheeler was elected to Congress. There, except for an interlude of a single month, he remained until 1900.

In Congress, Wheeler distinguished himself for his advocacy of sectional harmony. He supported pensions for Mexican War veterans and fought for the vindication of Federal General Fitz-John Porter, using both issues as occasions for reconciliation speeches. He followed the conservative wing of the Democratic party, clung to Cleveland despite his personal sympathy with free silver, and deplored the increasing strength of "populist" ideas in the Democratic ranks.

Upon the outbreak of the Spanish-American War, which he had steadily encouraged, he offered his services to President William McKinley. McKinley accepted; and Fighting Joe Wheeler, at sixty-three, became a major general of volunteers. He fought in Cuba, showing greater aggressiveness than most of the army commanders, and went briefly to the Philippines. Upon the close of the war, he became a brigadier general in the regular army. On his sixty-fourth birthday, September 10, 1900, he retired. In his last days he was one of the nation's more blatant jingoes and more ardent imperialists.

Fighting Joe Wheeler's career, moving from reconciliation to imperialism, marked perhaps the last phase of the leadership which the onetime leaders of

the Southern Confederacy gave to the Southern people. By the beginning of the twentieth century, most
of the old Confederacy's leaders were in their graves.
But those who remained and who had followed the
precepts of Robert E. Lee had evolved, as had Joseph
Wheeler, with the evolving nation. The wounds of
the war had healed, and a new nation was feeling its
strength. Into the fabric of the new nation were woven
the strong threads of the Confederate tradition.

Perhaps it was Brigadier General Edward Porter
Alexander who, among the surviving Confederate
leaders, best expressed the new sentiment—when on
"Alumni Day" in 1902 he spoke at West Point on
"The Confederate Veteran." General Alexander had
graduated from the military academy in 1857 and before the war had served there as an instructor. In the
Confederate service he had risen to be a brigadier
general, fighting at Gettysburg, at Knoxville, and in
the Wilderness. After the war, he had turned his
talents and energies to business and industry. He had
taught mathematics briefly at the University of South
Carolina and then had become president of the Columbia Oil Company. Successively, through the years,
he had been an actuary for an insurance company,
superintendent and then president of the Savannah
and Memphis Railroad, and president of the Central
Railroad and Banking Company of Georgia. He was
a writer of military history, a student of architecture,
a government director of the Union Pacific Railroad,

and an arbitrator of the boundary between Nicaragua and Costa Rica. He was well prepared by 1902 to speak of the Old South and of the New.

His words, or at least his tone, were reminiscent of General Longstreet's naïve and soldier-born concept that the highest law was that imposed by the sword. General Alexander's words were far more sophisticated but hardly different in meaning. The simple soldier had thought that under the ordeal of combat Southern principles had ceased to be principles. In 1902, General Alexander could voice the same thought in a new idiom.

"We believed," he told the West Pointers of a new generation, "that its sovereignty was intended to be reserved by each and every state" and that this was "divinely inspired wisdom." But what may have been wisdom "for that century," when each state was an independent agricultural community, was no longer valid. The railroad, the steamboat, and the telegraph had "made a new planet," and the old wisdom became "foolishness."

"Nature's great law of evolution," explained General Alexander, "against which no constitution can prevail, at once brought into play to overturn it forces as irresistible as those of a volcano." This was Darwinian evolution, and General Alexander proclaimed: "I . . . have discarded [old ideas] in favor of Darwinian theories. . . . I want conformation to environment. And as the changes in our planet still go

[145]

on, and as international commerce has grown up, a Siamese twin to national commerce, I applaud our nation's coming out of the swaddling bands of its infancy, and entering upon its grand inheritance. Let it stand for universal civilization. This is but a small and crowded planet, now that science has brought its ends together by her great inventions. Neither states nor nations can longer dwell to themselves. An irrepressible conflict is on between barbarism and civilization. Through human imperfection much that must be done may seem harsh and cruel. Much that has happened doubtless was so to our aborigines, but for all that we must look forward and not backward and walk boldly in the paths of progress. . . .

"As in 1865 one wicked hand retarded our unification by the murder of Lincoln, so in 1898 another assassin, equally wicked and equally stupid, by the blowing up of the *Maine,* has given us a common cause and made us at last and indeed a nation, in the front rank of the world's work of civilization, with its greatest problems committed to our care.

". . . the firm bonds which today hold together this great nation could have never been wrought by debates in Congress. Human evolution has not yet progressed so far. Such bonds must be forged, welded, and proved in the heat of battle, and must be cemented in blood. Peace Congresses and arbitrations have never yet given birth to a nation, and this one had to be born in nature's way."

Thus, with the martial achievements of Joseph Wheeler and the social Darwinism of Edward Alexander, the onetime leaders of the Confederacy had led the South into the new nation. The businessmen and the politicians who once had done battle for the agrarian South had followed the counsel of Robert E. Lee. They had rejected alike the political-collaboration doctrine of General Longstreet and the intransigence of President Davis, to work out a compromise by which the "results of the war" could be shared by Northerners and Southerners alike.

But in the end it was a compromise. It was not a complete surrender. General Alexander might seek for "conformity to environment" and co-operate in a New America that was becoming a world power, but the voices of Jefferson Davis, Albert Bledsoe, Moses Hoge, Benjamin Palmer, and Robert Louis Dabney still echoed in the Southland. They did not blend harmoniously with the clatter of the mining machinery of John C. Brown and the railroad whistles of T. M. Logan. There was discord still in Dixie. The Confederacy's leaders had not been united on secession, on the conduct of the war, or on the proper conduct to be followed after Appomattox. Their diverse views found lasting reflection in the conflicts which have remained, even to this day, in Southern life.